Turning from Truth

A NEW LOOK **AT THE GREAT APOSTASY**

Alexander B. Morrison

Turning from Truth

A NEW LOOK AT THE GREAT APOSTASY

Alexander B. Morrison

DESERET
BOOK

SALT LAKE CITY, UTAH

Library of Congress Cataloging-in-Publication Data

Morrison, Alexander B.
  Turning from truth : a new look at the great apostasy / Alexander B. Morrison.
    p. cm.
  Includes bibliographical references and index.
  ISBN 1-59038-395-8 (hardbound : alk. paper)
  1. Great Apostasy (Mormon doctrine) I. Title.
  BX8643.G74M67 2005
  270.1—dc22
                                                          2004022970

Printed in the United States of America   18961
R. R. Donnelley and Sons, Crawfordsville, IN

10 9   8   7   6   5   4   3   2   1

In memory of Elder Neal A. Maxwell,
dear friend and mentor, whose humble discipleship,
eloquent wisdom, and superb courage
inspired millions

OTHER BOOKS BY
ALEXANDER B. MORRISON

Dawning of a Brighter Day: The Church in Black Africa

Feed My Sheep: Leadership Ideas for Latter-day Shepherds

His Name Be Praised: Understanding Christ's Ministry and Mission

Valley of Sorrow: A Layman's Guide to Understanding Mental Illness

Visions of Zion

Zion: A Light in the Darkness

CONTENTS

PREFACE

THIS BOOK IS NOT AN OFFICIAL publication of The Church of Jesus Christ of Latter-day Saints. I was not asked to write it, and I alone am responsible for errors or omissions in the text. The ideas and views presented herein do not represent the position or views of the Church. They are mine, and I accept responsibility for them.

This book is not intended as a scholarly academic treatise on the subject of the Apostasy. I wrote it for the intelligent, non-specialist Latter-day Saint reader who wishes to understand the basic facts of the Apostasy but does not require an excessively academic text replete with a tedious flurry of footnotes and supposed scholarly detachment. Thus, I quote enough sources to make a point but do not feel compelled to quote everyone who ever commented on a given topic. Nor do I attempt to quote primary sources in the original language in which they were written. By reason of my inability to read either Greek or Latin, I have been forced to rely on those authorities whose works have been translated into English. In actuality, however, this has proven to be perhaps less of a hindrance than might at first be supposed.

The book starts from a simple premise, which is to me a self-evident truth: the two glorified Beings who spoke to the boy Joseph Smith on a spring morning in 1820 revealed a great truth when one of them said that the church He had established had been replaced by one which, while retaining some truth, had wandered far from the path and lacked divine approval.

I express deep gratitude to Professors Noel Reynolds, Andrew Skinner, David Paulsen, and John Gee of Brigham Young University, who read all or portions of the manuscript and gave me valuable suggestions and advice for corrections and alterations to it.

I acknowledge with gratitude the invaluable assistance of Afton Ferris, who somehow managed to decipher my written scrawl and, with unfailing cheerfulness and admirable accuracy, corrected it to a reasonable form.

Finally, I can never adequately acknowledge the love and support of my dear eternal companion, Shirley E. Morrison. She has encouraged and supported my efforts to write something meaningful with her usual patient, loving kindness. Her example inspires me to try to do better.

INTRODUCTION

THE CONCEPT OF A UNIVERSAL apostasy—a falling away from the truth of Christ's church as established by Him—is fundamental to the faith of the Latter-day Saints. Had an institutional apostasy not occurred, there would have been no need for a Restoration, no need for the Prophet Joseph Smith, no basis for Latter-day Saint claims that God has reestablished His church upon the earth, with necessary priesthood power and authority to carry out His work in ways fully approved by Him. In short, Mormonism, so-called, stands or falls, in major ways, on the reality of what Latter-day Saints commonly term "The Great Apostasy." In Elder James E. Talmage's inspired view, "If the alleged apostasy of the primitive Church was not a reality, The Church of Jesus Christ of Latter-day Saints is not the divine institution its name proclaims."[1]

It has been nearly a century since Elder James E. Talmage, later a member of the Quorum of the Twelve Apostles, wrote *The Great Apostasy,* in which he chronicled scriptural predictions that the church established by Jesus Christ would lose its divine authority to act in God's name, drift away from revealed truth,

1

and become an apostate organization. Elder Talmage also mar-
shaled impressive evidence that the primitive church had indeed
changed in significant ways that resulted in it becoming an organization whose beliefs and practices were fundamentally different
from those established by the Savior and His apostles. Central to
these changes was the loss of priesthood keys and authority
occurring after the death of the apostles and prophets who provided the necessary foundation for the church of Jesus Christ (see
Ephesians 2:20).

In his writings on the apostasy, Elder Talmage, in agreement
with earlier presentations by Elder B. H. Roberts, expressed the
view that the "darkness" of the medieval world provided evidence
of the dire effects of the apostasy. In his view, the light of the
Renaissance revival of learning set the stage for the Protestant reformation and, in turn, for the Restoration. [2]

Advances in modern scholarship over the last century have
shown that nineteenth-century views on the so-called Dark Ages,
though embraced by most historians of the period, require revision. The view that changes in the early church resulted in the
descent of a blanket of stygian darkness over the entire earth,
such that humankind had no contact with God or the Spirit for
nearly two millennia, simply doesn't stand up to the scrutiny of
modern scholarship. Scholars of today, benefiting from perspectives and information not readily available a century ago, understand that the "Dark Ages" were not nearly so dark as previously
had been thought. This assessment by an eminent twentieth-
century historian summarizes the contemporary view on this
subject:

"A few generations ago the medieval centuries of European
history were widely regarded as 'The Dark Ages.' Western man
was thought to have dropped into a deep slumber at the fall of
the Western Roman Empire in A.D. 476, awakening at length, like
Rip Van Winkle, in the bright dawn of the Italian Renaissance.

Indeed, it was the humanists of fifteenth-century Renaissance Italy who first created this dismal image of their medieval forebears, and the condemnation was echoed by the sixteenth-century Protestant reformers and by the philosophers of the eighteenth-century French Enlightenment. . . . [According to them] it was . . . a millennium of darkness—a thousand years without a bath.

"Today this ungenerous point of view stands discredited, although it persists among the half-educated. Several generations of rigorous historical scholarship have demonstrated that the medieval period was an epoch of immense vitality and profound creativity. The age that produced Thomas Aquinas and Dante, Notre Dame de Paris and Chartres, Parliament and the university, can hardly be described as 'dark' or 'barbaric.' . . .

"By the twelfth and thirteenth centuries Western Civilization had succeeded in attaining a cultural level comparable to that of the great civilizations of the past, but it also possessed an enormous potential for further development. It was destined, in later centuries, to transcend by far the achievements of the past and, for good or ill, transform the world."[3]

Furthermore, during the period of the so-called High Middle Ages—from about A.D. 1050 to 1300—European society now is recognized as having exhibited "demographic growth, religious reform, increasing political stability, and enormous economic development."[4] In short, it is a misnomer to apply the term "Dark Ages" to the period of time between the fall of the Roman empire and the Renaissance.

I hasten to point out that none of the recent advances in knowledge about earlier times has any impact on the validity of Elder Talmage's basic conclusion that a great apostasy from Christ's church occurred as the church departed from its apostolic roots. Indeed, what we now know only underlines the validity of Elder Talmage's assertions.

We must, however, conclude that mortals, illuminated by the
Spirit and the light of Christ—that which "giveth light to every
man that cometh into the world" (D&C 84:46)—still enjoyed at
least a measure of spiritual enlightenment and blessings during
the time between apostasy and restoration. Though bereft of
apostolic direction, there were many good men and good women
upon the earth during that long period of time—people who
strove with all their hearts to follow Christ and His teachings to
the best of their abilities. President John Taylor understood this.
He said:

"I have a great many misgivings about the intelligence that
men boast so much of in this enlightened day. There were men
in those dark ages who could commune with God, and who, by
the power of faith, could draw aside the curtain of eternity and
gaze upon the invisible world . . . , have the ministering of angels,
and unfold the future destinies of the world. If those were dark
ages I pray God to give me a little darkness, and deliver me from
the light and intelligence that prevail in our day."[5]

In writing this book, I want to emphasize that the world
owes a great debt to Christian churches, which kept the lamps of
civilization lit for so many years. In recounting the sad truths
of the Apostasy, we must take care not to be judgmental or self-
righteous, or to drive a wedge of contention between Latter-day
Saints and others. Elder Dallin H. Oaks expressed those senti-
ments as follows:

"We are indebted to the men and women who kept the light
of faith and learning alive through the centuries to the present
day. We have only to contrast the lesser light that exists among
peoples unfamiliar with the names of God and Jesus Christ to
realize the great contribution made by Christian teachers through
the ages. We honor them as servants of God."[6]

Many scholars agree that soon after its inception as a centrally
organized community under divine direction and apostolic

control, early Christianity became diverse and fragmented. By the second century of the Christian era, several varieties of Christianity had developed. Early Christianity existed in a complex religious, cultural, and political milieu, which both nurtured and transformed it. The complexity of Christian history and the sheer lack of definitive information about its crucial early years make it difficult at best to pinpoint the causes of the apostasy that Christianity underwent, to ascertain the changes which represent rejection of God's truth and rebellion against Him, and to determine the teachings and practices that remained true to those of Christ and His apostles. Some authorities believe, for example, that Augustine's fifth-century doctrine of original sin was heretical and that Pelagius' opposition to it was orthodox, and not the other way around. Be that as it may, Augustine's position eventually carried the day and became the official view of much of the Christian church.[7] Thus, it behooves anyone who approaches early church history to do so with humility and a certain amount of tentativeness. The record of first-century Christianity has large gaps. Almost no reliable documents from that period survived beyond those now included in the New Testament.

Furthermore, those who write about early church history must take care in deciding whose works they will read and which citations they will quote. The body of undisputed facts, though precious, is regrettably small and incomplete. There are many things we simply do not know and cannot verify from historical records. Facts and tradition often are mixed together in ways that make it difficult to separate them, and the data base not uncommonly is contradictory. It is seductively easy to "cherry-pick"—to choose a little here and a little there—to produce whatever conclusions the author wishes. Some historians of the period, who represent the "orthodox" views of Christian history, gloss over or ignore the gaping holes in what too often is presented as a seamless tapestry. Others fail to see the hand of God in anything and write early church history as though it were a purely secular matter. Still others are fascinated by the mysteries presented in apocryphal writings which, while intellectually titillating, have little doctrinal importance. Both care and prayer are needed if one is to do justice to this vitally important field.

Although the details of what happened and when are in numerous instances less than clear, we can be definitive about one basic fact: An apostasy from the primitive church *did* occur, with major effects on Western theology, culture, and history. That is sure and certain.

Before proceeding, it would be well to describe what is meant by "apostasy." The Greek word *apostasia,* from which its English equivalent, *apostasy,* is derived, means literally "to stand away" or "to stand against." It conveys the meaning of defection or revolt—a deliberate act of mutiny or rebellion. Apostasy thus occurs whenever an individual or community, having first received and accepted it, rejects the revealed word of God, rebels against His commandments and ordinances, and departs from the teachings of His authorized servants. The blessings of divine approbation and of authority to act in the name of God inevitably are lost, and sacred covenants are broken.

Professor James E. Faulconer of Brigham Young University notes that "we can justifiably speak of various kinds of apostasy, among them leaving the faith because of persecution, creating division in the body of the Church, losing faith because one continues to sin in various ways, teaching false doctrine, blaspheming, and denying the Holy Ghost. All of these can be summed up in one phrase, 'turning against God.' (See Hebrews 3:12.) To charge someone with apostasy is not to say that they have committed any particular sin. It is to say that person has turned his or her back to God."[8] Professor Faulconer also points out that "the Old Testament understanding of apostasy and, therefore, also [that of] the New, was that to be apostate was to turn against

God's covenant and, specifically, it was to refuse to stand before him in priesthood services."[9] Professor Faulconer concludes: "To apostatize is to sever one's connection to the priesthood."[10] In other words, the most grievous harm, amounting to a fatal injury, which results from apostasy is the loss of priesthood authority. Once the authority to speak as God's authorized agent, in His name, is lost, all else that is important soon will follow. When there is no longer a prophet to proclaim with authority, "Thus saith the Lord," the heavens withdraw, and divine approval is lost.

There is another aspect of apostasy that requires explanation. Latter-day Saints proclaim that human history has, from the beginning, been characterized by repetitive cycles involving the establishment of communities possessing priesthood authority, correct ordinances, covenantal relationships with God, and divinely approved doctrines and practices, followed by apostasy, repentance, and eventual revelatory restoration of truths and authority lost to the world. The cycle of faithful obedience, apostasy, repentance, and restoration, so evident in Nephite history, has been repeated over and over again throughout the ages. It is clear that throughout history, God has shared the gospel and the plan of salvation with His children, depending upon their receptivity and faithfulness. He stands ever ready, anxious to bless us, if we will but open the door to Him.

The Prophet Joseph Smith taught: "It is in the order of heavenly things that God should always send a new dispensation into the world when men have apostatized from the truth and lost the priesthood; but when men come out and build upon other men's foundations, they do it on their own responsibility, without authority from God; and when the floods come and the winds blow, their foundations will be found to be sand, and their whole fabric will crumble to dust.

Joseph Smith—

"Did I build on any other man's foundation? I have got all

the truth which the Christian world possessed, and an independent revelation in the bargain, and God will bear me off
triumphant."[11]

We Claim

The Church of Jesus Christ of Latter-day Saints proclaims
itself to be a revelatory restoration of divine truth and of authority to act in God's name. In Joseph Smith's first vision, he was
told by Jesus Christ that all existing churches at that time had
gone astray from the Savior's teachings, although they retained
"a form of godliness" (Joseph Smith–History 1:18–19). This
necessitated a restoration of knowledge and of priesthood authority, with its associated keys and covenants, to permit implemen-
tation of the Father's work and glory—which he has revealed is
to bring to pass the immortality and eternal life of His spiritually
begotten children (see Moses 1:39). God's "great plan of happiness" (Alma 42:8), the centerpiece of which is the atonement of
Jesus Christ, was, in fact, given to Adam, the "father of all"
(D&C 27:11), who stands as the head of the patriarchal order of
priesthood for this earth, under Christ (see Moses 5:4–12;
6:62–68). As a result of apostasy by Adam's descendants, this first
"dispensation" of the gospel did not last for very long. From time
to time, however, God, whose love for His children never wavers,
has created new dispensations, by calling new prophets, revealing
His plan for His children again to them, and bestowing necessary
priesthood authority on authorized servants.

It is important to note that the term *dispensation* denotes
both a period of time during which God has placed on the earth
necessary knowledge, priesthood, and keys of authority, *and* the
concept of stewardship over His work on the earth. In each dispensation, God's authorized servants act as His stewards, working as His agents, according to His orderly and revealed designs
for His children.

It is common, in some Latter-day Saint circles, to refer to
seven major gospel dispensations, each named after the most

important prophet thereof. Thus, some speak of the dispensa- _Dispensation?_ tions of Adam, Enoch, Noah, Abraham, Moses, Jesus Christ, and Joseph Smith. The dispensation led by Jesus Christ also is referred to as the dispensation of the "meridian of time," while that whose principal prophet is Joseph Smith commonly is known _Meridian of time_ as the dispensation of "the fulness of times." The list of seven dispensations must be considered partial at best. There undoubtedly have been other dispensations, such as those among the ten lost tribes of Israel, the Jaredites, and the Nephites.

Dispensations are intended to be universal, extending to all peoples everywhere, as were those of Adam (see Moses 5:12) and Abraham (see Abraham 2:11). More commonly, one people has been responsive to the gospel message while others have remained in ignorance, disbelief, and rejection of God. The final dispensation, the dispensation of "the fulness of times," is one wherein the gospel "shall be preached unto every nation, and kindred, and tongue and people" (D&C 133:37). Similarly, Jesus commanded His apostles to "go . . . into all the world, and preach the gospel to every creature" (Mark 16:15), but there is no evidence that commandment literally was fulfilled during the dispensation of the meridian of time.

The work of the Lord in each dispensation involves the same plan of redemption and salvation through faith in Jesus Christ. In other words, God reveals in each dispensation that which is required to fulfill His plans for His children. Part of the revealed plan in each dispensation, beginning with that of Adam, involves conferring to worthy men the power and authority of the holy priesthood, with its associated keys, ordinances, and covenants. Of course, differences may exist between dispensations with regard to revealed counsel and directions, as such are required in light of diversity in times and cultures. Thus, for example, blood sacrifices, required in Old Testament dispensations in similitude of the anticipated atonement of Jesus Christ, ended with the death and resurrection of the Savior. A new symbol of Christ's sacrifice for us was initiated by Jesus when He said to the Twelve, having taken bread and blessed it and broken it, "take, eat; this is my body. And he took the cup, and gave thanks, and gave it to them, saying, drink ye all of it; for this is my blood of the new testament, which is shed for many for the remission of sins" (Matthew 26:26–28; see also 1 Corinthians 11:23–25; 3 Nephi 20:8).

It must also be noted that the work of the Lord in each dispensation is open-ended. That which was not completed in an earlier dispensation, because of apostasy from the truth, will be finished during the final dispensation, appropriately labeled the "dispensation of the fulness of times." The final dispensation, which began with the restoration of the fulness of the gospel under the direction of the Prophet Joseph Smith, also will involve events unique to it, including the second coming of Jesus Christ and the Millennium.

The Prophet Joseph Smith, speaking of our day, taught that "truly this is a day long to be remembered by the Saints of the last days,—a day in which the God of heaven has begun to restore the ancient order of His kingdom unto His servants and His people,—a day in which all things are concurring to bring about the completion of the fullness of the Gospel, a fullness of the dispensation of dispensations, even the fullness of times; a day in which God has begun to make manifest and set in order in His Church those things which have been, and those things which the ancient prophets and wise men desired to see but died without beholding them; a day in which those things begin to be made manifest, which have been hid from before the foundation of the world, and which Jehovah has promised should be made known in His own due time unto His servants, to prepare the earth for the return of His glory, even a celestial glory, and a kingdom of Priests and kings to God and the Lamb, forever, on Mount Zion."[12]

Joseph Smith also taught that "the dispensation of the fullness of times will bring to light the things that have been revealed in all former dispensations; also other things that have not been before revealed. He shall send Elijah, the Prophet, [and others], and restore all things in Christ."[13]

The Prophet also noted that "all the ordinances and duties that ever have been required by the Priesthood, under the directions and commandments of the Almighty in any of the dispensations, shall all be had in the last dispensation, therefore all things had under the authority of the Priesthood at any former period, shall be had again, bringing to pass the restoration spoken of by the mouth of all the Holy Prophets."[14]

And from the latter-day revelations we read: "It is necessary in the ushering in of the dispensation of the fulness of times, which dispensation is now beginning to usher in, that a whole and complete and perfect union, and welding together of dispensations, and keys, and powers, and glories should take place, and be revealed from the days of Adam even to the present time. And not only this, but those things which never have been revealed from the foundation of the world, but have been kept hid from the wise and prudent, shall be revealed unto babes and sucklings in this, the dispensation of the fulness of times" (D&C 128:18).

The dispensation in which we now live is the last one prior to the second coming of the Savior. Unlike those that preceded it, it will not be destroyed by apostasy, though individuals, sadly, have continued and will continue to first accept and then reject God and rebel against Him. The unique status of this last dispensation is in fulfillment of Daniel's prophecy that "the God of heaven [will] set up a kingdom, which shall never be destroyed" (Daniel 2:44). President John Taylor reaffirmed this position when he

The Church will never be taken from the earth again

said: "This church [The Church of Jesus Christ of Latter-day Saints] fail? No! Times and seasons may change, revolution may succeed revolution; thrones may be cast down; and empires be dissolved; earthquakes may rend the earth from center to circumference; the mountains may be hurled out of their places, and the mighty ocean be moved from its bed, but amidst the crash of worlds and the crack of matter, truth, eternal truth, must remain unchanged, and those principles which God has revealed to his saints be unscathed amidst the warring elements, and remain as firm as the throne of Jehovah."[15]

It must be emphasized that simple differences of opinion do not, in and of themselves, constitute apostasy. Although free discussion and expression are encouraged in The Church of Jesus Christ of Latter-day Saints, there must, however, necessarily be limits thereto.

What is "personal apostacy" . . . Not differing in opinion

In 1869, Elder George Q. Cannon explained the limits of individual expression: "A friend . . . wished to know whether we . . . considered an honest difference of opinion between a member of the Church and the Authorities of the Church was apostasy. . . . We replied that . . . we could conceive of a man honestly differing in opinion from the Authorities of the Church and yet not be an apostate; but we could not conceive of a man publishing these differences of opinion and seeking by arguments, sophistry and special pleading to enforce them upon the people to produce division and strife and to place the acts and counsels of the Authorities of the Church, if possible, in a wrong light, and not be an apostate, for such conduct was apostasy as we understood the term."[16]

President James E. Faust, then a member of the Quorum of the Twelve, commented on individual apostasy as follows: "Those men and women who persist in publicly challenging basic doctrines, practices, and establishment of the Church sever themselves from the Spirit of the Lord and forfeit their right to place and influence in the Church. Members are encouraged to study the principles and the doctrines of the Church so that they understand them. Then, if questions arise and there are honest differences of opinion, members are encouraged to discuss these matters privately with priesthood leaders."[17]

Although the subject of this book deals with the general apostasy of the early church soon after Jesus' death and resurrection, these words of advice from wise priesthood bearers are worthy of note. Institutional apostasy *always* starts with *individual* apostasy.

Against that somewhat brief and sketchy background, let us begin to consider various aspects of the Great Apostasy, which shook and changed the early Christian church. We will do so by first outlining the social setting in which the infant church took root: the colorful cultural chaos of the Roman empire.

NOTES

1. Talmage, *The Great Apostasy*, iii.

2. See Roberts, *Outlines of Ecclesiastical History*, 121–228.

3. Hollister, *Medieval Europe*, 1–2.

4. McKay, et al, *A History of World Societies*, 331.

5. *Journal of Discourses*, 16:197.

6. Oaks, "Apostasy and Restoration," 85.

7. See Frend, *The Rise of Christianity*, 673–83.

8. Faulconer, "The Concept of Apostasy in the New Testament," 2–3.

9. Ibid., 25.

10. Ibid., 26.

11. *History of the Church*, 6:478–79.

12. *History of the Church*, 4:492–93.

13. *History of the Church*, 4:426; see also *Times and Seasons*, 15 October 1841, 578.

14. *History of the Church*, 4:210–11.

15. *Teachings of Presidents of the Church: John Taylor*, 85.

16. Cannon, *Gospel Truth*, 493.

17. Faust, "Keeping Covenants and Honoring the Priesthood," 38.

CHAPTER ONE

THE SOCIAL SETTING OF THE EARLY CHURCH

THE ROMAN EMPIRE, INTO WHICH the seeds of the Christian faith were sown, stretched from North Africa to Britain, from Spain to Asia Minor. Roman peace—the *pax romana*—prevailed throughout the broad lands. The frontiers were as yet secure, guarded by stalwart Roman legions who held the barbarian tribes of Central Asia and Northern Europe at arm's length. The great Augustus (Octavian) had brought peace to a war-torn world and planted the seeds of the golden age of the empire.[1] For fifty years after Augustus's death, the Julio-Claudian dynasty he founded provided the emperors of Rome. Some were capable and strong men, but two—Caligula and Nero—were weak, wicked, and capricious rulers, who brought sorrow and misery to all.[2] Nero persecuted the Christians in Rome (Peter and Paul probably were killed during this time), but his cruelties and stupidity led to military rebellion and his death in A.D. 68.[3] The Flavian dynasty, named after the clan of Vespasian,[4] the able soldier who restored order in Rome in A.D. 70, paved the way for the era of the "five good emperors,"[5] who oversaw the "golden age" of the empire (A.D. 96–180).

It was a time of almost unparalleled prosperity. Wars generally ended in Roman victories and were confined to frontier
regions far from the heartland of the empire. The Roman navy
had swept the sea of pirates. Brigandage was kept in check, and
the roads were relatively safe to travel. Britain, Gaul (France), the
Rhineland, and the lands of the Danube were opened to immi-
gration, much of it by retired legionnaires, who married local
women and settled where they had been garrisoned. Agriculture
flourished. Merchants traded extensively throughout the entire
empire: grain from Britain and Egypt; wool from Britain; olive
oil from Syria, Spain, and North Africa; wine, glass, and pottery
from Gaul; metals of all sorts from a dozen places, mingled with
silks, gems, spices, and perfumes from China and elsewhere in the
exotic East. Roman ships sailed from Egypt to the mouth of the
Indus River in India and beyond, reaching the Malay Peninsula,
Sumatra, and Java. The world had never seen anything like the
sweep of Roman influence before and would not again for
centuries into the future.

One of the outstanding features of the empire was that it
built and maintained great roads. The people of the Roman
empire traveled more extensively, more easily, and more safely
than anyone had before them, or would again until the nine-
teenth century. One authority has calculated that the Apostle
Paul, for example, traveled nearly 13,000 miles during his missionary journeys, much of it on foot.[6] The roads were filled with
traders, soldiers, government officials, runaway slaves, artisans,
teachers, and a multitude of others, speaking the dozens of languages of the empire. In part because the roads and sea lanes
were so good and safe, the peoples of the empire were much
more physically mobile than before or after these "golden years."

Artisans, traders, and craftsmen moved readily from one city
to another, carrying their tools with them. Arriving in a new city,
these skilled workers would have gravitated to neighborhoods

where others from their own ethnic or language group, trade, or culture already lived. For example, Priscilla and Aquila, whom Paul met in Corinth, had moved there from Rome after the emperor Claudius had commanded all Jews to leave that city (A.D. 48). Like Paul, they were tentmakers (see Acts 18:1–3). Later, they moved to Ephesus, traveling there with Paul (see Acts 18:18–19) before ending up again in Rome (see 1 Corinthians 16:19). Their final resting place may have been in Ephesus (see 2 Timothy 4:19); at least that is the last scriptural record of them. At some point, probably during their first stay in Ephesus, they became Christians, assisting in the conversion of Apollos, a Jew born in Alexandria (see Acts 18:24–26).

Another example of the ethnic and social diversity of the Roman empire is provided by the story of Lydia, a "seller of purple cloth" from Thyatira, in Asia Minor.[7] She met Paul in Philippi, in Macedonia (see Acts 16:12–14). Philippi was a Roman colony; it contained a body of Roman citizens, placed there for military purposes, and was governed directly from Rome, independent of provincial governments or local magistrates. As a businesswoman, Lydia would have traveled extensively, buying the purple cloth she sold, an especially prized commodity. She was probably wealthy. Lydia apparently was a Gentile who worshiped with Jews but was not a full convert to Judaism. She and her extended household were converted to Christianity and baptized, and her home became the home base for Paul's mission to Philippi (see Acts 16:40).

Wayne Meeks has pointed out that many early Christian meetings were held in private homes.[8] When Christians were fortunate enough to find someone who could offer a more spacious home, all groups of believers in a city might come together on occasion to worship and be instructed. Private homes offered numerous advantages: privacy from prying eyes of suspicious neighbors; a stable haven in which Christians could meet regularly; and probably physical protection as well. The grafting of Christian groups onto households, most of the members of which may have joined the church through baptism or at least may have been affiliated with it, clearly influenced patterns of church expansion in the early years of the Christian era.

Rome, the great imperial capital of the empire, was an extraordinary city by anyone's standards. It was huge, with a population somewhere between one-half to three-quarters of a million people in New Testament times. Its stately palaces, noble buildings, impressive monuments, and magnificent villas of the rich and influential contrasted with the squalor in which most of the people lived. The sponsorship of grandiose building projects in Rome came to be a normal part of imperial rule. Perhaps the most famous structure, the Colosseum, was built in A.D. 72–80 under the sponsorship of the emperors Vespasian and Titus. Rodney Stark has pointed out that most people who lived in the cities of the Roman empire were domiciled in tiny cubicles in multistoried tenements.[9] In his view, there were perhaps as many as 26 blocks of apartments, each four or five stories high, for every private house. Crowding was extreme, with whole families living in a single room and population densities approaching 200 per acre, similar to that in modern Bombay. Because there were neither furnaces nor fireplaces, cooking was done over wood or charcoal braziers in smoky rooms, made habitable (perhaps except on rainy days) by windows that were closed only by hanging cloths or skins over them. The dread of fire was an obsession. The tenements, made from flimsy building materials, also frequently collapsed under the weight of their inhabitants.

Not only were the people packed into tenement housing, but the streets themselves also were so narrow that one could almost literally shake the hand of the fellow across the street by leaning out the window. Even the famous roads that led out of Rome were only about 15 to 20 feet wide, and the streets in Rome were required by law to be only 9.5 feet wide. Needless to say, most people spent as much time as they could in the crowded streets, where at least they could mingle with their fellows, rather than be cooped up in the cramped quarters at home.

The crowding and squalor of the streets were compounded by the lack of sanitation. The water supply was contaminated with dangerous microorganisms and heavy metals. With no central sanitation systems—no sanitary or storm sewers—human waste was collected in chamber pots, which often were emptied out the window on the heads of unsuspecting passersby.

Crowding and lack of sanitation led to recurrent epidemics of infectious disease. The Roman historian Livy (59 B.C.–A.D. 17) recorded at least eleven pestilential disasters during the days of the Roman republic. [10] Another epidemic struck the city of Rome in A.D. 65, but a truly monstrous plague began spreading through the Roman empire a century later. This plague, probably introduced by soldiers who had been campaigning in Mesopotamia, remained at epidemic levels for fifteen years. It may have been smallpox, but a definitive diagnosis is simply not possible, given the state of medical knowledge at the time. Some experts believe that it may have killed one-third of the imperial population, or more.

From all that we know about the behavior of epidemics, and of the effects of crowding and lack of sanitation on the spread of disease in urban pestholes, it seems certain that mortality rates in the cities of the empire were high, especially among the poor, the young, and the old. The cities required constant and substantial influxes of newcomers just to maintain their populations at stable levels. As a result, they were populated by strangers who felt little attachment to most of their neighbors. Crime rates, one would expect, must have been very high in great cities fractured into numerous ethnic fragments, each suspicious and distrustful of the others.

Alexandria, founded by Alexander the Great in 332 B.C., was one of the most dynamic and sophisticated cities of the Roman empire.[11] Located on the Mediterranean Sea, and then, as now, a major port, it was a leading center of Hellenic scholarship. Alexandria was home to the most famous library of classical antiquity, the habitation of a people in love with Greek learning. There it was that the Septuagint, the Hebrew Bible read by Paul, was translated. There too stood the Pharos, the great 440-feet-tall lighthouse, which was one of the Seven Wonders of the World. Its vast lens, which magnified an oily fire, sent a beam that attracted the attention of ships of all nations from many miles at sea.

Alexandria contained vibrant communities of Greek, Egyptian, and Jewish people. Large numbers of thoroughly Hellenized Jews (perhaps as many as 25 percent of the one million Alexandrians) lived there, Greek not only in speech but in spirit. (By way of explanation, let me say that the Greeks call their land *Hellas*. Thus, the word *Hellenized* connotes a people who have adopted a wide range of Greek influence, including language, culture, outlook, art, etc.) At the beginning of the Christian era, Jews made up the majority in two of five districts in the city. Impressive numbers of early Christian leaders lived in Alexandria, including Clement of Alexandria, Origen, and Athanasius.

One of the most famous and largest cities in the Roman world was Antioch of Syria, on the river Orontes, 350 miles north of Jerusalem.[12] It was in Antioch that the disciples were first called Christians (see Acts 11:26). In common with great ports the world over, Antioch was a wicked and disreputable place. Today, the ancient city and its port have been silted up by the river and both lie under 30 feet and more of mud. Antioch was to the Romans a place of wild, exotic Eastern pleasures and sensual delights. Its chariot races were legendary, as was the volatility of the spectators. The main street of the city was two miles long, the first in the world to be paved with marble. It had been donated by the sycophant King Herod of Judea, in admiration of Augustus, the Roman Emperor.

Antioch's population came from every corner of the empire—Greeks, Romans, Syrians, and many others. There was a very large Jewish population, perhaps as much as 15 percent of the total, according to some authorities.[13] The Jewish historian Josephus[14] describes Jewish society at Antioch in the Apostle Paul's time:

"For as the Jewish nation is widely dispersed over all the habitable earth among its inhabitants, so it is very much intermingled with Syria by reason of its neighborhood, and had the greatest multitudes in Antioch by reason of the largeness of the city, wherein the kings, after Antiochus, had afforded them a habitation with the most undisturbed tranquility; for though Antiochus, who was called Epiphanes, laid Jerusalem waste and spoiled the temple, yet did those that succeeded him in the kingdom restore all the donations that were made of brass to the Jews of Antioch, and dedicated them to their synagogue; and granted them the enjoyment of equal privileges of citizens with the Greeks themselves. . . . They also made proselytes of a great many of the Greeks perpetually, and thereby, after sort, brought them to be a portion of their own body."[15] It was from Antioch that the Christian message entered the big cities of the Roman empire. But we have very few details of exactly how and when this happened. There was no written Christian history at that time. The book of Acts and later church tradition are all that is available.

But one thing seems certain: Christianity, from the time of Paul onward, was primarily an urban movement. Though Jesus had preached to the people of the small villages and rural landscapes of Judea and Galilee, His apostles preached almost entirely to city folk, perhaps in part because there were many more who lived in the cities than in the countryside. Though economic ties between urban and rural centers were necessarily close, the two worlds, throughout history, have not been friends. City dwellers have tended to look upon country folk as uneducated, loutish bumpkins, while their rural counterparts have seen city dwellers as arrogant, money-gouging "slickers" who, unlike their rural brethren in Roman times, paid few, if any, taxes.

Not only were the cities of the Greco-Roman world where the money and power were, they were also places where social and religious changes were most likely to occur. Urban dwellers traditionally have been less conservative than their rural counterparts, perhaps in part because rural life has always been so physically exhausting, so close to the line in terms of survival, that change has been a risk that could not be indulged. Young men and women of ambition and drive have tended throughout history to migrate to the cities to seek their fortunes. And it was in the cities of the Roman empire—in Antioch, Ephesus, Alexandria, Corinth, and Rome—that Peter, Paul, and their associates found audiences prepared to listen to and embrace the Christian message.

There is a long-standing myth that Christianity became the religion of the "dregs of the populace, of peasants and mechanics, of boys and women, of beggars and slaves."[16] But there is considerable evidence that in the first century, Christianity spread primarily in the urban circles of middle-class artisans, merchants, and professionals.[17] Christianity was *not* primarily a movement of the dispossessed, of slaves and peasants, housekeepers and cooks, those from the lower classes. Available evidence indicates that its members represented "a fair cross-section of [Roman] urban society."[18] Of course, there were many "peasants and mechanics, boys and women, beggars and slaves" who were Christian, but that simply reflects the predominance of such people in Roman society. To be sure, Paul had noted that "not many wise men after the flesh, not many mighty, not many noble, are called: But God hath chosen the foolish things of the world to confound the wise; and God hath chosen the weak things of the world to confound the things which are mighty" (1 Corinthians 1:26–27). But that is not to say that *none* of the worldly wise, mighty, and noble were chosen, just "not many." Simply put, there were not very many such in Roman society; indeed, there are not all that many, in percentage terms, in our present world either.

We do know that some people of considerable substance and social standing became Christians early on. Erastus, the city treasurer at Corinth and a very prominent citizen, was a Christian (see Romans 16:23; 2 Timothy 4:20). Marta Sordi, professor of Greek and Roman history at the Catholic University of Milan, states that "we know from reliable sources that there were Christians among the [Roman] aristocracy in the second half of the first century . . . and that it seems probable that the same can be said for the first half of the same century, before Paul's arrival in Rome. . . . The Roman Christians met for worship in the houses of patricians [persons of high birth] who were either converts to the new religion, or who in any case felt friendly towards it."[19] Sardi also mentions Pomponia Graecina, a woman of the Roman senatorial class, who became a Christian as early as A.D. 42, and protected her faith from prying eyes by explaining her way of life during the forty years she was a Christian as being "in mourning for a friend."[20] And in truth she was!

In Paul's letter to Philemon, we learn that Philemon was a slaveholder in Colossae, a small city east of Ephesus, and was therefore probably wealthy. He also had a house big enough that church meetings were held there.

In summary, therefore, there is considerable evidence that early Christianity was largely a middle-class movement. In fact, Rodney Stark, drawing from his sociological background, suggests that early Christianity, if it behaved like other new religions for which there is sound information, may actually have over-recruited persons of more privileged backgrounds.[21] Stark is, however, careful to point out (and we would do well to heed his cautions) that we cannot "prove" that the early church had "its greatest appeal to the solid citizens of the [Roman] empire,"[22] any more than we can prove, in an empirical sense, much else about early Christianity.

JEWS IN THE ROMAN EMPIRE

As previously mentioned, many Jews lived in Antioch and Alexandria. But there were also large Jewish communities in virtually every city and town of the empire. Many—perhaps five or six million—were Jews of the Diaspora, more or less permanently settled outside of Judea after the Babylonian exile and successive foreign conquests of Palestine. But others were Jews who voluntarily migrated to various places in search of improved economic circumstances for themselves and their families. This mobility was a direct result of the relatively unrestricted movements of peoples within the Roman empire.

We can expect, as with other immigrant groups, that the Jews joined with others of their faith to continue their familiar religious practices, enjoy relationships with family members and friends, settle internal disputes with other Jews, and lobby for better treatment of themselves and their co-religionists. Some aspects of their religious beliefs, including their sense of exclusivity, kept them apart from non-Jews and aroused concerns among the Roman authorities and dominant groups in the local societies in which they lived. As a result, there was always tension between Jews and non-Jews, and Jewish relationships with the larger community were always ambivalent at best. Though they shared some rights with Roman citizens, Jews were never quite accepted. Their perennial demands for guarantees that they would not have to violate Sabbath observance or dietary laws, or practice idolatry, irritated and offended others. But the Jews understood that their identity—the maintenance of the covenant between Abraham and God—required that they keep strong boundaries between themselves and others. On the one hand, their strong sense of communal unity, coupled with vigorous pursuit of economic advancement and general high moral standards, engendered respect from many. But others, frightened by supposed and often exaggerated reports of Jewish wealth and numbers, were resentful and jealous.

Jews were simultaneously tugged and torn in two directions. They were pressured to conform to Greco-Roman culture, and many were deeply attracted to it. Greek—not Hebrew—was their common language and many were culturally, at least, more Greek than Jew. But they also were pressured to remain separate from non-Jews, to be faithful to their cherished traditions. It was not an easy task. The difficulty of living in two worlds and not being fully accepted by either is illustrated by the life of the Apostle Paul, who was by birth both a Jew and a citizen of Rome, yet was sent by his father to Jerusalem to study with the great rabbi Gamaliel (see Acts 16:37; 21:20; 22:3, 25–29). Torn between being a Jew and a Roman, Paul was torn again: he first persecuted Christians and then became one of their greatest champions.

The question of whether Jews could possess the rights of citizenship was finally settled by the Emperor Claudius in A.D. 41, at least for Jews in Alexandria.[23] A copy of his directive was discovered in the early twentieth century. In it, Claudius confirmed the Jews' rights to continue their ancestral customs without molestation but flatly denied them the right to be considered Roman citizens. The legal benefits they already enjoyed would have to suffice. The legal situation in other cities is not known, but probably was not much different, though local practices (as compared to law) might have either ameliorated or exacerbated the plight of the Jews elsewhere in the empire.

HELLENIZATION

As Alexander the Great lay dying in Babylon in June of 323 B.C., his friends, gathered around his bedside, asked him a vital question—to whom would he bequeath his kingdom? The dying man whispered, "To the strongest."[24] Alexander was a conqueror and a destroyer, not a builder. The empire he built began to fall apart the moment he was gone. No single commander could hold his vast conquests together. Brutal civil war soon ensued, and peace came only when the Romans conquered the lands of the eastern Mediterranean approximately a century and a half before Christ.

But the practical result of Alexander's conquests was to open the East to the spread of Greek influences. Large numbers of Greeks migrated to newly established cities throughout the lands conquered by Alexander—to Egypt, Asia Minor, Mesopotamia, and beyond. Greek writers and artists brought Greek culture with them. Architects, skilled craftsmen, engineers, bureaucrats, and builders were in great demand. Whole cities sprang into existence. In Egypt, for example, bustling provincial cities were established as commercial agribusinesses, part of huge irrigation and farming schemes that flourished for centuries in African oases, until their fields salted up and were abandoned.[25] The crops they produced were shipped to Rome and elsewhere in the empire. Each settlement was a Hellenistic microcosm, with Greek, Egyptian, and Jewish cultures all mixed together, living cheek by jowl in uneasy relationships. Each city would have had a Greek *agora* (market), extensive bath-houses, perhaps a gymnasium, a theater, a temple for various Greco-Egyptian gods. From the vast detritus of such cities has come an incredible variety of ancient texts, including the most famous of all, a tiny remnant of papyrus on which is found, in Greek (of course), the earliest known fragment of New Testament writing. Known as the Rylands Fragment, it is a tiny snippet from the gospel of John, dealing with Jesus' trial before the Jewish Council, and includes Pilate's cynical statement, "What is truth?" (John 18:38). Authorities believe it was written about A.D. 130, around a century after Jesus' crucifixion and a full century before the oldest known relatively complete texts of books of the New Testament as we know them were prepared. The Rylands Fragment probably came from a Christian meeting house, but we will never know for sure. [26]

The Greek language (not Latin) became the common language of educated people in the whole Greco-Roman world from North Africa to Asia Minor, Syria, Mesopotamia, even as far east as the Indian subcontinent. Anyone who wanted to compete in business or to rise in the army or secular bureaucracy had to learn it. Men and women of ambition sought to become Greek in soul as well as speech. The Apostle Paul spoke and wrote fluent Greek, and the Hebrew scripture he read, the Septuagint, was written in Greek, reportedly in Alexandria two centuries or more before Paul's time.

Greek-speaking traders spread their laws and trading practices throughout the East. Caravans linked China to the Mediterranean world, and luxury goods (silks, jewels, precious metals, spices, etc.) flowed into Greece, Italy, and Spain. Greek styles of pottery and glassware, of furniture, sculpture, and painting, even city planning and literary style, were ubiquitous throughout the Greco-Roman world.

The Greeks and Easterners (i.e., non-European inhabitants of the Roman empire) shared their religious traditions without much difficulty, each assuming they were worshiping the same gods with different names. Greek religious cults were attractive

to many ambitious Easterners who adopted Greek culture to help
with personal advancement socially or in business. But Greek religions did little to satisfy deep religious feelings or spiritual yearn-
ings. The Greeks began to adopt various Eastern "mystery" religions, which featured rituals and practices not to be divulged to
those not initiated into the group. Two Eastern cults that were
wildly popular in the Hellenistic world were from Egypt. One
involved the Egyptian god Serapis, a sort of combination of
Osiris (from Egypt) and Zeus, Pluto, and Asclepius (from
Greece). Serapis was believed to be a judge of souls who
rewarded virtuous people with eternal life. The cult of Isis, the
wife of Osiris, was even more popular, especially among women
who believed that she was the goddess of marriage, conception,
and childbirth, the founder of law and literature.[27]

The Hellenistic world encompassed a time of spiritual seeking and a growing desire for spiritual answers to the inherent
uncertainties and trials of life. Schools of philosophers, including
those of the Cynics, the Epicureans, and the Stoics, were prominent.[28] But even they did not soothe the longings of heart and
soul, which many still felt, to know the truth. The Hellenized
peoples to whom the Christian gospel was brought were in many
instances receptive to it. But beginning toward the end of the
second century they attempted to rationalize the gospel with
Greek philosophy, beliefs, and lifestyles. A great battle arose for
men's hearts and minds. As Professor Stephen E. Robinson has
noted, "The Greeks' world-view eventually won, and Jewish
Christianity was revised to make it more attractive and appealing
to a Greek audience."[29]

RELIGION IN THE ROMAN EMPIRE

The Romans believed that the welfare of the state depended
upon the favor of the "eternal gods." If the legions won a battle,

it was because the gods were pleased; if they lost, the gods had been offended by the carelessness of those who should have paid them proper homage. So too famine, flood, plague, or economic distress were caused by neglecting the gods, who were not being properly worshiped through appropriate prayer and sacrifices in the temples.

In the Roman world, the state was careful not to deny the existence of the gods of any religion and did not claim there was one true religion. After all, why take a chance? Better to be respectful of all, just to be sure. Within limits, therefore, people were free to worship whatever and however they wished, so long as their practices did not threaten the peace, well-being, and unity of the empire. To that extent, there was religious toleration. It is important to note that the Roman state did not really care what people believed. That was a private matter, governed by one's own personal philosophy and of no concern of the state. To the Romans religion was a matter of ritual and virtually nothing else.

The various religions within the empire were regulated by the Roman government, through an official called the *Pontifex Maximus* (chief priest), to ensure that there was no friction between them, or at least that such was kept within tolerable bounds. The various shrines and temples found throughout the empire also were maintained by the Roman government, and financial assistance was given to the various religious cults.

Edward Gibbon described the place of religion in the empire: "The various modes of worship, which prevailed in the Roman world, were all considered by the people, as equally true; by the philosopher, as equally false; and by the magistrate, as equally useful. And thus toleration produced not only mutual indulgence, but even religious concord."[30] Cynical certainly, but largely true: the empire and its leaders were more concerned about using religion as a unifying force than about esoteric details of personal salvation or whether one religion was true and another false.

There were literally hundreds of religious cults in the empire, but overlaying them all was emperor worship. The personage of the emperor came to be considered as an embodiment of the favor of the "eternal gods" toward the empire, and the emperor himself was thought to be a god. The purpose of emperor worship had nothing to do with salvation or eternal life. Its purpose was to demonstrate one's loyalty to the state, not unlike pledging allegiance to the flag. Providing that was done, with appropriate respectful sacrifices at the altars in the temples, the authorities, as already noted, cared little about what people actually believed. Loyalty made for obedient citizens and blessed peace. So long as peace and unity were maintained, what people believed beyond that was of little concern or consequence to the state. However, those who refused to make the proper sacrifices in the prescribed way showed a regrettable disloyalty and were considered to be atheists.

In addition to the prescribed worship of the emperor, the pledge of allegiance, so to speak, hundreds of other deities were also worshiped locally. For example, Artemis protected Ephesus, and Apollo favored Delphi. Proper worship of the local deities, it was believed, brought blessings to fields and orchards and protected one's city or neighborhood from misfortune. If the legions lost a battle on some far-flung frontier, emissaries were sent to identify the local god who had been offended. Once found, he or she would be brought over to the Roman side by appropriate ceremonies, which incorporated the previously unknown god into the pantheon of gods of the empire.

Since neither emperor worship nor the worship of state or local deities provided the hope and solace to heart and soul so eagerly sought by so many, people had their own individual or household deity to whom they paid obeisance. Included in that category were many gods of "mystery" cults, coming from Greece, Egypt, or Persia, which promised salvation to initiates in possession of special, secret knowledge.

In addition, all classes, races, crafts, and trades had their own deity. The silversmiths of Ephesus, for example, worshiped Artemis (Diana), as Paul found out (see Acts 19). Indeed, a given individual might simultaneously worship the emperor, a local deity, and the god of his or her own personal choice.

There was a remarkable synchronization of gods in the Roman world. The names of Greek deities commonly were changed when they became Roman. For example, the Greek Artemis became the Roman Diana; the Greek Hephaestus became the Roman Vulcan; Ares of Greece became the Roman Mars; and Hermes, the Greek messenger-god, became the Roman Mercury.

Why, it might be asked, could not the Christians just fit into this polytheistic world, worshiping just another of the multitude of gods acceptable to Rome? The answer was simple, yet profound: Christians refused to worship the emperor, and they could not and would not worship "the eternal gods" of Rome. Christianity was exclusionist in nature. To Christians, there was but one God, the Eternal Father, whose Son, a manifestation of the Supreme Being in the flesh, had come to earth, died for men's sins, was resurrected, and now sat exalted in the presence of the Father. Unlike the pagan religions of the empire, which required ritual acts and little else, Christianity was a religion of beliefs. To Christians, the essence of true religion was what one thought about God and mankind's relationship to Him. As Jesus said, "And this is life eternal, that they might know thee the only true God, and Jesus Christ, whom thou hast sent" (John 17:3).

Christianity therefore became an illicit and outlawed religion, existing outside of the protection and recognition of the *Pontifex Maximus,* with no rights to hold property, construct buildings, or hold worship services. Since its scripture contained the Old Testament, and many of its earliest members had been Jews, many Romans considered Christianity to be nothing more than a Jewish sect. Therefore, Christians often were swept up in the periodic persecution of Jews in the Roman empire.

But amidst all of the cultural chaos of the Roman empire, amidst all of the wars and troubles Christians faced, we should not underestimate the impact of the new religion on the behavior of its adherents. Justin Martyr, called "the philosopher," a prominent Christian convert who embraced Christianity circa A.D. 130 and was martyred in Rome circa A.D. 165, wrote about the joy of his new life and of how Christianity had changed him:

"We, out of every tribe of people . . . who used to take pleasure in promiscuity, now embrace chastity alone; we, who once had recourse to magic, dedicate ourselves to the good God; we, who valued above everything else acquiring wealth and possessions, now bring what we have into a common fund, and share with everyone in need; we who hated and killed other people, and refused to live with people of another tribe because of their different customs, now live intimately with them."[31]

NOTES

1. See McKay, et al., *A History of World Societies,* 157–63.
2. Ibid., 165.
3. Ibid.
4. Ibid., 166.
5. Ibid. The "five good emperors" were Nerva, Trajan, Hadrian, Antoninus Pius, and Marcus Aurelius.
6. See Anderson, *Understanding Paul,* 16.
7. *The Eerdmans Bible Dictionary,* s.v. "Lydia," 669.
8. See Meeks, *The Moral World of the First Christians,* 111.
9. See Stark, *The Rise of Christianity,* 147–62.
10. See McNeill, *Plagues and Peoples,* 103–9.
11. See Frend, *The Rise of Christianity,* 34–37.
12. See Romer, *Testament,* 187–88.

13. See Anderson, *Understanding Paul*, 34.

14. Josephus was a Jewish political and military leader who went over to the Roman side during the Roman sack of Jerusalem in A.D. 70. His accounts provide much valuable information on Jewish history during the first century A.D.

15. Josephus, *The Wars of the Jews*, in *The Works of Josephus*, 753.

16. Gibbon, *The History of the Decline and Fall of the Roman Empire*, 2:142.

17. See Stark, *The Rise of Christianity*, 29–33.

18. Meeks, *The First Urban Christians*, 73.

19. Sordi, *The Christians and the Roman Empire*, 28–29.

20. Ibid., 29.

21. See Stark, *The Rise of Christianity*, 46.

22. Ibid., 45.

23. See Frend, *The Rise of Christianity*, 37.

24. Green, *Alexander of Macedon, 356–323 B.C.*, 475.

25. See Romer, *Testament*, 185.

26. Ibid., 183–85.

27. See McKay et al., *A History of World Societies*, 138.

28. The Cynics, whose most famous spokesman was Diogenes (circa 412–323 B.C.), advised people to live simply, discarding traditional customs. The Epicureans believed the gods had no effect on human life; individuals could obtain serenity and peace by rejecting the world and ignoring politics. Zeno (335–262 B.C.) founded the school of thought called Stoicism. The Stoics believed that all people are brothers, governed by one natural law. Achievement counts for little; what is important is a virtuous life. Stoic philosophy was influential in formulation of the Roman view of a universal state governed by natural law.

29. Robinson, "Warring Against the Saints of God," 39.

30. Gibbon, *The History of the Decline and Fall of the Roman Empire*, 1:53.

31. Quoted in Pagels, *Beyond Belief*, 13.

CHAPTER TWO

THE PROPHETS WARN OF APOSTASY TO COME

THE SAVIOR JESUS CHRIST MOURNED the fact that after His mortal ministry men had rebelled against the truth and had established their own forms of worship. In a revelation given to the Prophet Joseph Smith on 1 November 1831, the Lord declared of an apostate world: "They have strayed from mine ordinances, and have broken mine everlasting covenant; they seek not the Lord to establish his righteousness, but every man walketh in his own way, and after the image of his own god, whose image is in the likeness of the world, and whose substance is that of an idol, which waxeth old and shall perish in Babylon [i.e., the apostate, wicked world], even Babylon the great, which shall fall" (D&C 1:15–16).

Christ's reference to "the everlasting covenant" brings to mind the prophecy of Isaiah, who beheld in a vision a time of spiritual darkness and confusion, when the earth itself seemed to mourn, desecrated, spiritually empty and wasted: "The earth also is defiled under the inhabitants thereof; because they have transgressed the laws, changed the ordinance, broken the everlasting covenant" (Isaiah 24:5). What does the term "everlasting covenant" mean? The "everlasting covenant" is the gospel of Christ, ordained by Him who is Everlasting. Salvation is attained by adherence to its laws and ordinances. What is the relationship between the "everlasting covenant" and the Law of Moses? When the earth mourns in spiritual darkness, is it the Law of Moses that has been broken? It seems unlikely. The Mosaic Law is nowhere referred to in scripture as an "everlasting covenant." "The law," taught Paul, "was our schoolmaster to bring us unto Christ, that we might be justified by faith. But after that faith is come, we are no longer under a schoolmaster. For ye are all the children of God by faith in Christ Jesus. For as many of you as have been baptized into Christ have put on Christ" (Galatians 3:24–27; see also 2 Nephi 25:30; Mosiah 13:27; Alma 25:16). In other words, the Mosaic Law was intended to be superseded by something higher, to be replaced by the gospel of Christ, with its centerpiece His atoning sacrifice. Indeed, Paul refers to Christ's atoning blood, which was shed for all mankind, as "the blood of the everlasting covenant" (Hebrews 13:20). Breaking the "everlasting covenant" must therefore refer to a future state, when the Law of Moses no longer applies to Israel, and when the "everlasting covenant" of Christ's sacrifice has been broken by apostasy. That indeed is what happened.

Within twenty-five years of Christ's resurrection, the dark stain of apostasy was beginning to creep into the infant church. The Apostle Paul warned of divisions and internecine strife, which were beginning to tear at the very vitals of the community of Saints. To the Saints at Corinth—a notoriously wicked place even by the lax standards of the time—Paul lamented: "Now I beseech you, brethren, by the name of our Lord Jesus Christ, that ye all speak the same thing, and that there be no divisions among you; but that ye be perfectly joined together in the same mind and in the same judgment. For it hath been declared unto me of you, my brethren, by them which are of the house of

Chloe, that there are contentions among you. Now this I say, that every one of you saith, I am of Paul; and I of Apollos; and I of Cephas; and I of Christ. Is Christ divided? was Paul crucified for you? or were ye baptized in the name of Paul?" (1 Corinthians 1:10–13). Diversity, pride, contention, dissimulation, factionalism—all are the hallmarks of beginning rebellion against God, of a church sliding into apostasy. Paul knew that unless such was stemmed, unless those involved repented of their sins and turned away from them in forgiveness of others, joining hands with their brethren and sisters in the fellowship of Christ, the church would tear itself apart. Sadly, they did not return to the true path, and apostasy was the result.

It is of interest to note that Clement, a bishop of Rome late in the first century, confirmed the sad state of the church in Corinth. He characterized the Corinthian church as afflicted by "emulation, and envy, and strife, and sedition: persecution, and disorder, war and captivity. So they who were of no renown lifted up themselves against the honourable; those of no reputation against those that were in respect; the foolish against the wise, the young men against the aged. Therefore righteousness and peace are departed from you, because every one hath forsaken the fear of God, and is grown blind in his faith, nor walketh by the rule of God's commandments, nor liveth as is fitting in Christ; but every one follows his own wicked lusts, having taken up an unjust and wicked envy, by which death first entered into the world."[1]

On his way back from Greece to Jerusalem, Paul stopped at Miletus, south of Ephesus, where he gave a tearful farewell address to "the elders of the church." The apostle was full of foreboding, knowing as he did that the apostasy was at hand, as had clearly been prophesied. "For I know this, that after my departing shall grievous wolves enter in among you, not sparing the flock." (Here Paul speaks metaphorically; the wolves represent apostate deceivers.) The apostle continued: "Also of your own selves shall men arise, speaking perverse things [i.e., false doctrine that incites rebellion], to draw away disciples after them. Therefore watch, and remember, that by the space of three years I ceased not to warn every one night and day with tears" (Acts 20:29–31). Paul knew that the gravest dangers to the church were internal and that the near future would bring betrayal, disobedience, corruptions, perversion, rebellion, and denial of the truth.

But it was not only the Saints in the area around Ephesus who were at peril. Some time, probably prior to his last visit to Jerusalem in A.D. 58, Paul wrote to the Saints in Galatia, an area in the center of Asia Minor, including perhaps the towns of Antioch of Pisidia, Iconium, Lystra, and Derbe, visited by Paul on his first missionary journey. Paul's letter to the Galatians was written in response to the news of a wholesale defection from the infant church in the form of a return to Jewish law, with the severe limitations it imposed on spiritual advancement. "I marvel that ye are so soon removed from him that called you into the grace of Christ unto another gospel: which is not another; but there be some that trouble you, and would pervert the gospel of Christ" (Galatians 1:6–7).

To emphasize the perilous position of those who sought to pervert the gospel of Christ, the apostle continued: "But though we, or an angel from heaven, preach any other gospel unto you than that which we have preached unto you, let him be accursed. . . . O foolish Galatians, who hath bewitched you, that ye should not obey the truth, before whose eyes Jesus Christ hath been evidently set forth, crucified among you?" (Galatians 1:8; 3:1).

Problems had been brewing for some time between Gentile and Jewish converts to Christianity. On the one side were those who, believing they had been purchased with the blood of Christ (see Acts 20:28), did not feel required to obey the dead letter of a dead law. On the other side were those only partially converted Jewish Christians who considered it necessary to still follow the Mosaic Law with its multitudinous, nit-picking requirements. The latter were Christian in name, but largely Jewish in act and belief. (We will discuss the Ebionites, a Jewish-Christian heretical sect, in more detail in chapter 8.) A major issue was the question whether all converts to Christianity should be circumcised as well as baptized. Had such been agreed, Christianity would have become at best a reform movement within Judaism. Expansion of the church among the Gentiles would, for practical purposes, have been impossible. Such of course could not occur, if the gospel were to be preached, as Jesus had commanded, "to every creature" (Mark 16:15).

At the Council of Jerusalem, probably held before A.D. 58, though that date cannot be verified with certainty, the presiding Brethren, Peter, James, and John, set the future course for the church by proclaiming, under the influence and direction of the Holy Ghost, that Gentile converts need not be circumcised, but should observe Mosaic prescriptions concerning acceptable foods and sexual behavior.

But that battle within the church was not yet over. "Judaizers"—those only partially converted to Christ and Him crucified, still uncertain about His virgin birth, still believing it essential to keep the Law of Moses—continued to plague the church for decades. Indeed, as Sidney B. Sperry noted, "Those of us in the Church today have had little conception of the difficulties that faced the Authorities of the Early Church with respect to this problem."[2] Sperry was of the view that the dissension caused by the Judaizers was "one of the things that helped in the end to split the Church wide open and to bring about the 'Great Apostasy.'"[3]

In the long run, however, the cause of the Jewish party within Christendom failed, and by the end of the first century A.D., Jews and Christians clearly had gone their separate ways, though small groups of Jewish-Christians continued to exist for several centuries. [4]

Paul's letters to the Saints in Thessalonica are considered to be the earliest of his epistles, dating perhaps from early in the sixth decade of the Christian era. The spirit of iniquity was already abroad in the church. The false belief that "the day of Christ is at hand"—that the second coming was at the very door—evidently was widespread. Paul dealt with that erroneous notion in his usual forthright manner: "Be not soon shaken in mind, or be troubled, neither by spirit, nor by word, nor by letter as from us, as that the day of Christ is at hand" (2 Thessalonians 2:2). The Joseph Smith Translation of that verse reads as follows: " . . . be not shaken in mind, nor be troubled by letter, except ye receive it from us; neither by spirit, nor by word, as that the day of Christ is at hand" (2 Thessalonians 2:2 a). Paul is saying to the Thessalonians, in effect: "Wake up, stop daydreaming about the future. Christ will come when He comes. Stop worrying and fretting over it. Strengthen your own faith; deal with the apostasy, the rebellion against God, which is your real threat."

The apostle goes on: "That day [i.e., the day of Christ's second coming] shall not come, except there come a falling away [i.e., apostasy] first, and that man of sin be revealed, the son of perdition; who opposeth and exalteth himself above all that is called God, or that is worshipped; so that he as God sitteth in the temple of God, showing himself that he is God. Remember ye not, that, when I was yet with you, I told you these things?" (2 Thessalonians 2:3–5). The man of sin is of course Satan, the grand deceiver, the malignant mastermind of wickedness.

Most of the Christian world accepts the prophecy that widespread rebellion against God will indeed occur, but believes that will happen just before Christ's second coming. But there is no basis for believing in such a long delay. Paul goes on to say that "the mystery of iniquity *doth already work*" (v. 7, emphasis added). Evil is already at the door, he says: the threat is *now*, not in some undetermined future.

The phrase "mystery of iniquity" is an interesting one. Many of those who perverted the simple truths of Christ's gospel were attracted to mystery cults, including Gnosticism and other heretical movements, which pretended to give their adherents access to "special" knowledge restricted to only a few, but ended up by dissembling, deceiving, and destroying the unwary.

Furthermore, Paul's reference to the man of sin, the son of perdition, sitting in the temple of God, refers not to the Jerusalem temple of Paul's day, as many of our Christian brethren believe (and which in any case would be destroyed in just twenty more years), but (allegorically) to the church of Christ. In other words, Satan will for a season take over—occupy, if you will—the church, and with "signs and lying wonders," will destroy those that "received not the love of the truth, that they might be saved" (ibid., vv. 9–10).

Paul's other letters also convey his deep concern for the future of the church, which he wore out his life serving and building. Examples include the following:

To the Ephesians: "Have no fellowship with the unfruitful works of darkness" (Ephesians 5:11).

To the Philippians: "Beware of dogs, beware of evil workers, beware of the concision" (Philippians 3:2). (Note: *Concision* means "cutting into pieces, separating, mutilation.")

To the Colossians: "Beware lest any man spoil you through philosophy and vain deceit, after the tradition of men, after the rudiments of the world, and not after Christ" (Colossians 2:8).

To Timothy: "In the latter times some shall depart from the faith, giving heed to seducing spirits, and doctrines of devils" (1 Timothy 4:1).

To Titus: "For there are many unruly and vain talkers and

deceivers . . . whose mouths must be stopped, who subvert whole houses, teaching things which they ought not, for filthy lucre's sake" (Titus 1:10–11).

To the Hebrews: "Therefore we ought to give the more earnest heed to the things which we have heard, lest at any time we should let them slip" (Hebrews 2:1).

It seems clear from Paul's writings that much of the apostasy resulted from internal rebellion within the church itself, from its members who for whatever reason turned against the truth.

Paul's second letter to his beloved Timothy reveals the depth of the troubles that had beset the infant church. "This thou knowest," Paul wrote, "that all they which are in Asia be turned away from me" (2 Timothy 1:15). The Roman province of Asia included Ephesus, Colossae, and Laodicea, cities in which Paul had preached and to which he sent letters. What sorrow, even perhaps despair, is conveyed by those words. Paul must have feared that his life's work had been in vain, his trials and tribulation for nought. One senses Paul recognized that the storm that was already sweeping through the church would not subside before it had taken a terrible toll: "For the time will come when they will not endure sound doctrine; but after their own lusts shall they heap to themselves teachers, having itching ears; and they shall turn away their ears from the truth" (2 Timothy 4:3–4).

Jude, traditionally identified as one of Jesus' half-brothers (see Matthew 13:55), who wrote his epistle approximately sixty years after Jesus' death and resurrection, complained that "there are certain men crept in unawares, who were before of old ordained to this condemnation, ungodly men, turning the grace of our God into lasciviousness, and denying the only Lord God, and our Lord Jesus Christ. . . . These filthy dreamers defile the flesh, despise dominion, and speak evil of dignities [and] . . . speak evil of those things which they know not: but what they know not naturally, as brute beasts, in those things they corrupt themselves. . . . These are spots in your feasts of charity, when they feast with you, feeding themselves without fear: clouds they are without water, . . . murmurers, complainers, walking after their own lusts; and their mouth speaketh great swelling words, having men's persons in admiration, because of advantage [profit or gain]" (Jude 1:4, 8, 10, 12, 16). Pride, contention, evil-speaking, sexual immorality, unbridled sensuality—such are the hallmarks of a growing apostasy. The church of Christ cannot be built or maintained upon such foundations.

Some modern scholars believe that the Apostle John wrote his gospel, at least in part, to counteract apostate teachings by heretical Gnostics, who preached the abominable falsehood that the Spirit of God had descended on a mortal man (Jesus) at His baptism.[5] Thus, to emphasize Christ's eternal existence, John wrote, "In the beginning was the Word, and the Word was with God, and the Word was God. The same was in the beginning with God" (John 1:1–2). John wrote his first epistle sometime between A.D. 70 and 100, in response to the threat of the Gnostic heresy. In it the apostle testified that he had personally seen, heard and touched the Savior (see 1 John 1:1–3). Jesus was real, not a phantom as the Docetic Gnostics falsely averred.[6]

Peter's second epistle again records the well-worn list of evidences of apostasy: "There shall be false teachers among you, who privily shall bring in damnable heresies, even denying the Lord that bought them, and bring upon themselves swift destruction. And many shall follow their pernicious ways; by reason of whom the way of truth shall be evil spoken of. And through covetousness shall they with feigned words make merchandise of you: whose judgment now of a long time lingereth not, and their damnation slumbereth not. . . . The Lord knoweth how to deliver the godly out of temptations, and to reserve the unjust unto the day of judgment to be punished: but chiefly them that walk after the flesh in the lust of uncleanness, and despise government. Presumptuous are they, self-willed, they are not afraid to speak evil of dignities. . . . Having eyes full of adultery, and that cannot cease from sin; beguiling unstable souls: an heart they have exercised with covetous practices; cursed children: which have forsaken the right way, and are gone astray" (2 Peter 2:1–3, 9, 14–15).

There they are again, the same old faults and failings: pride, contention, rebellion, unwillingness to take counsel and direction, sexual immorality. How the faithful apostles must have worried whether some people are too perverse, too gullible, or too willful to ever follow the truth for very long.

Let us, then, summarize the faults and failings that the prophets have warned lead individuals to reject God, to mutiny against the Almighty, to corrupt His teachings, to defect from His cause. Taken as a whole, they delineate the internal contention that was a major cause of the apostasy of the early church. Indeed, a persuasive case can be made that the self-inflicted wounds of dissent and discord were at the very center of the internal rebellion which changed the church.

Human nature being what it is, there should be little wonder that without the constraint that comes from God, the church should evolve into something quite different than the Lord intended. For scriptural references on this topic, see the Appendix.

In considering the ease with which apostasy swept through the early church, it is well to keep in mind the practical difficulties under which the early apostles had to work. Persecution, mistrust, and suspicion on the part of neighbors and legal authorities were common. In spite of it all, little branches of the church, with, initially at least, only a few members in each, were established by the apostles and their associates throughout Asia Minor, and eventually southern Europe and northern Africa. But spiritually speaking, the members were still as babes. The gospel they had embraced required major changes in themselves—not only in what they believed but in how they behaved.

Furthermore, at the beginning there were no written collections of the teachings of Jesus for guidance, inspiration, and instruction of the faithful. There was no general conference with talks that strengthen, sustain, and, as needed, correct the understandings of the members; no satellite broadcasts; no written word of prophetic advice and counsel; no cadre of experienced, faithful priesthood and sister leaders to stabilize and help build up local units. Letters addressing practical problems faced by the Saints were written by Paul and others, but lacking a state-run postal service, it must have taken a long time to hand-deliver the epistles to their recipients. It was a much different world from that of today, and we know relatively little about much of what went on. The records simply are missing, as we will discuss in more detail later.

Perhaps the most striking impression that comes from this brief summary of prophetic warnings is that this apostasy, by and large, came from inner spiritual decay—from rebellion within the ranks of church members. This turning from truth was an act of mutiny, aided and abetted, no doubt, by the forces of evil. Pride; contention; fault-finding; envy; disunity; love of power; unwillingness to take counsel, even from the apostles and prophets; unbridled sensuality—these were the sins that propelled the ancient church into apostasy. Sadly, they are the same sins that continue to buffet the Saints—and humanity in general—in our day. There are important lessons to be learned from that lamentable truth. We must always be on the alert, always striving to stay as far as we can on the Lord's side of the line that separates good from evil in life. The Prophet Joseph Smith stated a great truth when he said:

"The Messiah's kingdom on earth is of that kind of government, that there has always been numerous apostates, for the reason that it admits of no sins unrepented of without excluding the individual from its fellowship. Our Lord said, 'Strive to enter in at the straight gate; for many, I say unto you, will seek to enter in, and shall not be able.' And again, many are called, but few are chosen. Paul said to the elders of the Church at Ephesus, after he had labored three years with them, that he knew that some of their own number would turn away from the faith, and seek to lead away disciples after them. None, we presume, in this generation will pretend that he has the experience of Paul in building up the Church of Christ; and yet, after his departure from the Church at Ephesus, many, even of the elders, turned away from the truth; and what is almost always the case, sought to lead away disciples after them. Strange as it may appear at first thought, yet it is no less strange than true, that notwithstanding all the professed determination to live godly, apostates after turning from the faith of Christ, unless they have speedily repented, have sooner or later fallen into the snares of the wicked one, and have been left destitute of the Spirit of God, to manifest their wickedness in the eyes of multitudes. From apostates the faithful have received the severest persecutions. Judas was rebuked and immediately betrayed his Lord into the hands of His enemies, because Satan entered into him. There is a superior intelligence bestowed upon such as obeyed the Gospel with full purpose of heart, which, if sinned against, the apostate is left naked and destitute of the Spirit of God, and he is, in truth, nigh unto cursing, and his end is to be burned. When once that light which was in them is taken from them they become as much darkened as they were previously enlightened, and then, no marvel, if all their power should be enlisted against the truth, and they, Judas like, seek the destruction of those who were their greatest benefactors. . . . From what source emanated the principle which has ever been manifested by apostates from the true Church to persecute with double diligence, and seek with double perseverance, to destroy those whom they once professed to love, with whom they once communed, and with whom they once covenanted to strive with every power in righteousness to obtain the rest of God? Perhaps our brethren will say the same that caused Satan to seek to overthrow the kingdom of God, because he himself was evil, and God's kingdom is holy."[7]

One of the most deadly expressions of the apostasy was a loss of priesthood authority and the end of apostolic direction. Those losses both caused and were the result of rebellion against God. We will now consider these most fundamental of all losses in the infant church.

NOTES

1. "Epistle of Clement of Rome," in *The Apostolic Fathers*, 1:160.
2. Sperry, *Paul's Life and Letters*, 208.
3. Ibid., 59.
4. See Frend, *The Rise of Christianity*, 91–92.
5. See Pagels, *Beyond Belief*, 72–73.
6. See chapter 8 of this book.
7. *History of the Church*, 2:22–23.

CHAPTER THREE

LOSS OF PRIESTHOOD AUTHORITY: THE DEADLIEST INJURY

IT IS IRONIC TO NOTE THAT WE KNOW least about the details of the most important part of the puzzle of the Apostasy. I refer, of course, to priesthood authority and apostolic direction, the power to operate in God's name and with His authority. Once divine authority and direction were lost, it was only a matter of time until the church slid inexorably and inevitably into apostasy. In the absence of priesthood authority, nothing else matters very much, in terms of the retention of divine approbation. Under inspired priesthood direction, on the other hand, appropriate course corrections can be made as needed. Priesthood authority is the anchor that ties any church claiming to be authorized by God to its Rock and Salvation. Continuing revelation to divinely accepted servants, "legal administrators," as some have termed properly authorized priesthood leaders who bear the keys to direct the work of God on earth, is *the* essential characteristic of His church. Authority acceptable to God to preach the gospel and administer in the ordinances thereof can be conferred upon a worthy man only by prophecy and the laying on of hands by those who are in authority (see Article of Faith 4). More than good will or righteous desires is required. A holy ordinance must be performed, and it must be administered in a specific way by one who has divine authority to do so. As Paul said, "No man taketh this honour unto himself, but he that is called of God, as was Aaron" (Hebrews 5:4). At some point, early in the history of the infant church, that essential chain linking God and man was broken.

It must be noted at the onset that in the absence of priesthood authority the channels of revelation, which flow from God to His prophets, were fatally disrupted. Inspiration, which can guide good men and women everywhere, and the light of Christ, "which lighteth every man that cometh into the world" (John 1:9), could not take the place of revealed knowledge insofar as leadership of the church goes.

In an address given only six weeks before his martyrdom, the Prophet Joseph Smith noted that "a man can do nothing for himself unless God direct him in the right way; and the priesthood is for that purpose."[1] Just over a week before he was martyred, the Prophet amplified those remarks: "It is in the order of heavenly things that God should always send a new dispensation into the world when men have apostatized from the truth and lost the priesthood; but when men come out and build upon other men's foundations, they do it on their own responsibility, without authority from God; and when the floods come and the winds blow, their foundations will be found to be sand, and their whole fabric will crumble to dust."[2]

That is precisely what happened in the ancient church: priesthood authority and the revelation associated with it were lost, probably some time late in the first or early second century A.D., and men began to build upon their own foundations. By this time, Christianity had become fragmented, with numerous local organizational and doctrinal manifestations. In the absence of unity in doctrine and practices, the church soon lost its linkage to the Divine. Regardless of the virtue of the people who directed it—and that attribute varied all the way from good to evil, over the centuries—the church, though it retained a form of godliness and became a powerful force in the world, was no longer the church of Jesus Christ. We cannot escape that ineluctable fact.

Hegesippus, the second-century Jewish-Christian writer (see note 11) says that until the time of the Emperor Domitian (A.D. 81–96), "the Church had remained a virgin, pure and uncorrupted, since those who were trying to corrupt the wholesome standard of the saving message, if such there were, lurked somewhere under cover of darkness. But when the sacred band of the apostles had in various ways reached the end of their life, and the generation of those privileged to listen with their own ears to the divine wisdom had passed on, then godless error began to take shape, through the deceit of false teachers, who now that none of the apostles was left threw off the mask and attempted to counter the preaching of the truth by preaching the knowledge falsely so called."[3]

But I return to an earlier theme: though the church, bereft of apostolic direction, lost divine approval and was no longer the Church of the Lamb, there was still plenty of goodness in the people who called themselves Christians, both amongst ordinary folk and their leaders. J. B. Phillips caught the spirit of that goodness and desire to do God's will in his description of the early church:

"Yet we cannot help feeling disturbed as well as moved, for this surely is the Church as it was meant to be. It is vigorous and flexible, for these are the days before it ever became fat and short of breath through prosperity, or musclebound by overorganization. These men did not make 'acts of faith,' they believed; they did not 'say their prayers,' they really prayed. They did not hold conferences on psychosomatic medicine, they simply healed the sick. . . . We in the modern Church have unquestionably *lost* something. Whether it is due to the atrophy of the quality which the New Testament calls 'faith,' whether it is due to a stifling churchiness, whether it is due to our sinful complacency over the scandal of a divided Church, or whatever the cause may be, very little of the modern Church could bear comparison with the spiritual drive, the genuine fellowship, and the gay [i.e., joyful] unconquerable courage of the Young Church."[4]

In our assertion that the church had apostatized, we must *not* conclude that all virtue had left the world. We must *not* for even a moment think that with the apostasy a blanket of spiritual darkness, keeping out all light and truth, descended upon humankind, suffocating and choking off every good and worthy thought and deed, erasing Christ from every heart. That just didn't happen, and we do a grave injustice to all Christians, including ourselves, if we think otherwise. Indeed, I think it true that, in some ways at least, mainstream Christian denominations are weaker *now*, after the Restoration, than the church was three centuries after Christ. In our day, faith has given way not just to disbelief but to active and organized ridicule of spirituality; carnality, in all its debauched manifestations, rules supreme; and men call good evil and evil good on all sides.

Why all this emphasis on priesthood authority? Is the priesthood restricted to only a select elite, such that it is vocational or hereditary, or is it a "priesthood of all believers," as in the Protestant view? To all aspects of that question we, the Latter-day Saints, would answer "no." What then is priesthood anyway? The Prophet Joseph Smith answered that question: "The Priesthood is an everlasting principle, and existed with God from eternity, and will to eternity, without beginning of days or end of years. The keys have to be brought from heaven whenever the Gospel is sent."[5]

President Gordon B. Hinckley has commented on the nature of priesthood as follows:

"What is this remarkable gift and power that has come to us with no price other than our personal worthiness? . . .

"It [the priesthood] is veritably the power of the Almighty given to man to act in His name and in His stead. It is a delegation of divine authority, different from all other powers and authorities on the face of the earth. Small wonder that it was restored to man by resurrected beings who held it anciently, that there might be no question concerning its authority and validity. Without it there could be a church in name only, lacking authority to administer in the things of God. With it, nothing is impossible in carrying forward the work of the kingdom of God. It is divine in its nature. It is both temporal and eternal in its authority. It is the only power on the earth that reaches beyond the veil of death. Said the Lord to His chosen Apostles: 'And I will give unto thee the keys of the kingdom of heaven: and whatsoever thou shalt bind on earth shall be bound in heaven: and whatsoever thou shalt loose on earth shall be loosed in heaven.' (Matt. 16:19.) . . .

"In its ultimate expression the holy priesthood carries with it the authority to seal on the earth and have that sealing effective in the heavens. It is unique and wonderful. It is the authority exercised in the temples of God. It concerns both the living and the dead. It is of the very essence of eternity. It is divine power bestowed by the Almighty as a part of His great plan for the immortality and eternal life of man.

"How precious is the gift of God that has come to us."[6]

Priesthood, then is *power*—the power of God, the power by which the cosmos was put in place and worlds without number were organized. By this power the gospel is preached with authority, and sacred ordinances required for the exaltation of both the living and the dead are performed. Through the priesthood revelation is obtained, conveying to His children God's mind and will.

Priesthood is also *authority*—the right to act in the name of God, to serve as His authorized agent upon the earth. It is the authority to perform saving and exalting ordinances and have them ratified and upheld in the heavens.

Finally, priesthood is the *right and responsibility to preside,* within the organizational structure of the church of Jesus Christ, to direct God's work on earth. The power to direct the work of the priesthood is referred to as the keys of the priesthood. Those keys are given to priesthood bearers who are called to preside over priesthood quorums, functions, or organizational divisions of the Church. Priesthood power can be exercised only in righteousness. Indeed, the power and authority of the priesthood in general cease to exist in a man if they are used to obtain the honors of the world, to gratify pride or ambition, to exercise unrighteous dominion over others, or to cover up sin (see D&C 121:37). I aver that personal apostasy in the early church, characterized by contention, disunity, power-grabbing, pride, and all the other sins of mortality, led to a loss of priesthood authority. And that doomed the church, insofar as divine approbation is concerned.

The Apostle Paul noted that the priesthood foundation of the household of God includes "apostles and prophets, Jesus Christ himself being the chief corner stone; in whom all the building fitly framed together groweth unto an holy temple in the Lord" (Ephesians 2:20–21). In other words, where the kingdom of God is found, there will be found apostles and prophets. The reverse also is true; a church without apostles and prophets is not—whatever else it may be—the church of Jesus Christ.

In the New Testament, apostles (from the Greek *apostellein,* to send forth, as an authorized agent or as an ambassador) were divinely chosen and ordained servants. To His twelve apostles, Jesus said, "Ye have not chosen me, but I have chosen you, and ordained you, that ye should go and bring forth fruit, and that your fruit should remain: that whatsoever ye shall ask of the Father in my name, he may give it you" (John 15:16). Initially, Jesus chose twelve apostles from "[those] men which have companied with [Him] all the time that the Lord Jesus went in and out among us" (Acts 1:21). The names of the original Twelve are given in scripture. Although there are some differences in the gospel accounts, Matthew lists them as "the first, Simon, who is called Peter, and Andrew his brother; James the son of Zebedee, and John his brother; Philip, and Bartholomew; Thomas, and Matthew the publican; James the son of Alphaeus, and Lebbaeus, whose surname was Thaddaeus; Simon the Canaanite, and Judas Iscariot who also betrayed [Jesus]" (Matthew 10:2–4). The number twelve echoes the number of tribes of Israel whom the apostles are to judge (see Matthew 19:28; Luke 22:30).

Apostles hold the keys of the priesthood, the authority to direct the work of the church of Jesus Christ in all the world. In The Church of Jesus Christ of Latter-day Saints the keys, while held by all apostles, are fully operative in the hands of only one man, the senior apostle, who also is the president of the Church. President Harold B. Lee noted that "the Lord has said to Joseph Smith what he said to Peter and what he has said to every prophet in every dispensation. He gives to each the keys to the kingdom of heaven, and the power to receive revelation in order that the gates of hell shall not prevail against his plan."[7]

After the suicide of Judas Iscariot, who had betrayed Jesus Christ, it was necessary to fill the resultant vacancy in the Quorum of the Twelve. Luke describes the process involved: "And they appointed two, Joseph called Barsabas, who was surnamed Justus, and Matthias. And they prayed, and said, Thou, Lord, which knowest the hearts of all men, shew whether of these two thou hast chosen, that he may take part in this ministry and apostleship, from which Judas by transgression fell, that he might go to his own place. And they gave forth their lots; and the lot fell upon Matthias; and he was numbered with the eleven apostles" (Acts 1:23–24).

But then the scriptural and historical records quickly begin to fade away. There clearly were apostles called who are not known to have been among the Twelve, including Paul and Barnabas (see Acts 14:14; 1 Corinthians 9:5–6). Paul referred to himself repeatedly as an apostle (see Romans 1:1; 1 Corinthians 1:1; 9:1; Galatians 1:1), and it appears that by about A.D. 54 James "the brother of the Lord" was also an apostle (see 1 Corinthians 15:7; Galatians 1:19), but whether Paul, Barnabas, and James "the brother of the Lord" were members of the Quorum of the Twelve is not known, though they probably were.

And then, after about A.D. 90, the record goes suddenly and completely dark. Peter and Paul probably were killed just prior to or during the Neronian persecution (A.D. 64), but what happened to the other apostles lies in the realm of tradition and legend, unverifiable by what is known today. Bereft of its apostolic direction, the church could not long survive as one with divine authority.

Many mainstream Christian denominations assert that the apostolic succession—namely, from Jesus to the Twelve, and from them to others, not called apostles but appointed by them—has been maintained by an unbroken series of bishops, each handing power and authority to his successor.

Ignatius of Antioch, martyred probably in Rome in A.D. 107, insisted that local bishops were the focus of unity in the church. He claimed "the bishop is God's representative on earth, the earthly counterpart [of Christ himself], so that 'we ought to regard the bishop as the Lord himself.'"[8]

However, Ignatius recognized that bishops, of which he was one, are not apostles. In his epistle to the Trallians, he wrote, "Let all reverence the deacons as Jesus Christ; and the bishop as the Father; and the presbyters [elders] as the sanhedrim [sic] of

God, and college of the apostles. Without these there is no church." Then, tellingly, he wrote, "I will not write any more sharply unto you about this matter . . . lest, being a condemned man, *I should seem to prescribe to you as an apostle.*"[9] Ignatius, though a bishop (in Antioch), was careful not to overstep the bounds of his authority. He was no apostle, and he knew it.

The idea of the unique role of bishops as successors to the apostles proved valuable in counteracting heretical claims, primarily from Gnostic sects, that Jesus had imparted secret knowledge to the apostles during the forty days of His ministry after the Resurrection. It still remains an unverified and unverifiable claim, however, nothing more. It is the only defense available to churches that must assert episcopal succession to prove their own validity. Thus, it is claimed that in such churches bishops perform the functions of the apostles (they do not); their commission goes back to the apostles (there is no evidence of such); they succeed each other in the same geographical areas occupied by the original apostles (there is no evidence of such); and they inherit from the original apostles the transmission of the Holy Ghost which empowers them for the performance of their work.[10] Frankly, all of these claims are unverifiable, and do not hold up to even superficial scrutiny. There is no hint of bishops in anything said by Jesus in the Gospels. Claims of an unbroken line of succession from the current pope to Peter, supposedly the first bishop of Rome, for example, are highly suspect, to say the least. W. H. C. Frend notes there is no trace in what he terms the "subapostolic" period (the period of time following the death of the original apostles) of a single bishop in Rome, with full authority for the church there and elsewhere in Christendom prior to the time of Hegesippus[11] (circa A.D. 175).[12] In other words, the supposed chain of episcopal succession does not exist, or at least cannot be proven to exist, before A.D. 175.

The idea of episcopal succession may be likened to a relay

race, where each authorized team member in turn passes off the baton to the next in line. If any runner drops the baton, for whatever reason, his team is finished. The race is over for them. That surely happened over and over again, during the history of the papacy, as unrighteous men "dropped the baton," so to speak.

It is telling that the claim of validity offered by the generation of leaders after the apostles was not "I was ordained by one who had authority from God," but rather "I knew the apostle _____ (fill in the blank)." Claims to have known Peter or Paul or another apostle say little about the worth of the speaker, and the story gets even thinner the further one gets from the original writers.

Furthermore, there is no scriptural evidence, or valid historical evidence either, as to the specific geographic areas opened up for the Christian cause by the ancient apostles. We simply do not know which churches they "founded."

Tradition asserts that Peter and Paul founded the church at Rome, the city where both probably were martyred.[13] That seems improbable, since in Paul's letter to the Romans (written about A.D. 58) he sends greetings to an already established church in Rome and hopes that "by the will of God" he might visit them (Romans 1:10). Significantly, Paul makes no mention of Peter, though he sends greetings to a large number (28) of other Christians already in Rome (see Romans 16). Surely he would not have neglected to send greetings to Peter, the chief apostle, had Peter been in Rome. By the third century, it had become politically advantageous for "orthodox" Christians to promote the idea of an unbroken line of leaders to an illustrious early founder. Doing so provided a pedigree of "orthodoxy" to counteract the teachings of heretical groups such as the Gnostics and Montanists.[14]

Additionally, the behavior of many of the bishops of traditional Christian churches over the centuries hardly qualifies them for receipt of the gift of the Holy Ghost. Barbara Tuchman, the eminent historian, has pointed out that from roughly A.D. 1470 to 1530, six popes, from Sixtus IV to Clement VII, carried the papacy to "an excess of venality, amorality, avarice, and spectacularly calamitous power politics. Their governance dismayed the faithful, brought the Holy See into disrepute, left unanswered the cry for reform, . . . and ended by breaking apart the unity of Christendom."[15] For an even more graphic description of excesses by medieval bishops of Rome, readers may wish to refer to William Manchester's book, *A World Lit Only by Fire*.[16]

Johann Lorenz von Mosheim, a famous ecclesiastical historian whose work has been characterized as exhibiting unprecedented objectivity and penetration, has chronicled the excesses of third-century bishops that seem incompatible with retention of the gift of the Holy Ghost, or of approbation from the Almighty. He wrote: "Though several yet continued to exhibit to the world illustrious examples of primitive piety and Christian virtue, yet many were sunk in luxury and voluptuousness, puffed up with vanity, arrogance, and ambition, possessed with a spirit of contention and discord, and addicted to many other vices that cast an undeserved reproach upon the holy religion, of which they were the unworthy professors and ministers. This is testified in such an ample manner, by the repeated complaints of many of the most respectable writers of this age, that truth will not permit us to spread the veil, which we should otherwise be desirous to cast over such enormities among an order so sacred. The bishops assumed, in many places, a princely authority, particularly those who had the greatest number of churches under their inspection, and who presided over the most opulent assemblies. They appropriated to their evangelical function the splendid ensigns of temporal majesty; a throne, surrounded with ministers, exalted above his equals the servant of the meek and humble Jesus; and sumptuous garments dazzled the eyes and the minds of the multitude into an ignorant veneration for this usurped authority. An example which ought not to have been followed, was ambitiously imitated by the presbyters, who, neglecting the sacred duties of their station, abandoned themselves to the indolence and delicacy of an effeminate and luxurious life. The deacons, beholding the presbyters thus deserting their functions, boldly invaded their rights and privileges; and the effects of a corrupt ambition were spread through every rank of the sacred order."[17]

Finally, the office of bishop, as understood by the Latter-day Saints, while almost entirely a local and not a general office, does not carry with it under any circumstances the apostolic keys and authority (see page 55) needed to guide the whole of the kingdom of God. Bishops simply cannot legally appoint their own successors, a practice that was already in place (complete with the most venal politicking) by the end of the second century.

Once apostolic authority and direction were no more, and men were left to their own devices, it should not surprise us that the sacred ordinances and the covenants always associated with them also underwent change. To the Prophet Joseph Smith the Lord declared, speaking of our contemporary world, "For they [the inhabitants of earth] have strayed from mine ordinances, and have broken mine everlasting covenant" (D&C 1:15).

Woe be unto those who tamper with the sacred ordinances. Yet tampering is just what happened. Let us consider the ordinance of baptism as a case in point. The baptism by immersion of Jesus by John the Baptist set the divinely approved pattern for the future administration of this sacred ordinance (see Mark 1:9–11). In the early church, candidates were baptized on their acceptance of the gospel message (see Acts 8:35–39). By the beginning of the third century, however, formal instruction, sometimes lasting up to three years, was required before baptism. The period for preparing candidates for baptism before Easter became formalized into the forty days of Lent. By that time baptism, though usually still by immersion, required the candidate to confess faith in each member of the Trinity, with immersion after each of the three confessions. Gregory, bishop of Rome from A.D. 590 to 604, approved a single immersion, but some Eastern churches have preserved the practice of immersing the candidate for baptism three times.

The precedent of Jewish washings (see Leviticus 14–15), circumstantial accounts of baptism in the early Christian literature, and the symbolism of baptism as burial and resurrection (see Romans 6:1–11) suggest strongly that, in the early church, baptism involved complete immersion, or dipping of the entire person. However, by the second century, the *Didache*,[18] a manual of church life included among the works of the Apostolic Fathers, permitted pouring water three times on the head instead of complete immersion.

The earliest extant reference to infant baptism is from about the year A.D. 200; infant baptism seems at that time to have been a relatively new practice. By the fifth century, infant baptism was common; it received great impetus from the doctrine of original sin propounded by Augustine[19] and was decreed by church councils in the medieval period. Early Christian documents, in contrast, contain frequent references to the sinlessness of children. Furthermore, the word of the Lord on the matter, given to the prophet Mormon, is as follows: "I came into the world not to call the righteous but sinners to repentance; the whole need no physician, but they that are sick; wherefore, little children are whole, for they are not capable of committing sin; wherefore the curse of Adam is taken from them in me, that it hath no power over them; and the law of circumcision is done away in me" (Moroni 8:8).

Speaking further on the baptism of children, Mormon explained:

"And after this manner did the Holy Ghost manifest the word of God unto me; wherefore, my beloved son, I know that it is solemn mockery before God, that ye should baptize little children.

"Behold I say unto you that this thing shall ye teach—repentance and baptism unto those who are accountable and capable of committing sin; yea, teach parents that they must repent and be baptized, and humble themselves as their little children, and they shall all be saved with their little children.

"And their little children need no repentance, neither baptism. Behold, baptism is unto repentance to the fulfilling the commandments unto the remission of sins. But little children are alive in Christ, even from the foundation of the world; if not so, God is a partial God, and also a changeable God, and a respecter to persons; for how many little children have died without baptism!

"Wherefore, if little children could not be saved without baptism, these must have gone to an endless hell.

"Behold I say unto you, that he that supposeth that little children need baptism is in the gall of bitterness and in the bonds of iniquity; for he hath neither faith, hope, nor charity; wherefore, should he be cut off while in the thought, he must go down to hell.

"For awful is the wickedness to suppose that God saveth one child because of baptism, and the other must perish because he hath no baptism.

"Wo be unto them that shall pervert the ways of the Lord after this manner, for they shall perish except they repent. Behold, I speak with boldness, having authority from God; and I fear not what man can do; for perfect love casteth out all fear" (Moroni 8:9–16).

It is impossible to imagine a more strongly worded, emphatic statement on this topic.

More extensive information on baptism in the early Christian church is found in *The Eerdmans Bible Dictionary*[20] and in the *Encyclopedia of Early Christianity*.[21]

The doctrine of the sacrament, as it is known by Latter-day Saints, or the Eucharist, as most other Christians call the bread and wine (or water) offered "in remembrance of Jesus" (see 1 Corinthians 11:23–26) also has undergone significant changes over the years. In A.D. 1215 the Fourth Lateran Council[22] of the Roman Catholic Church affirmed that in some mystical manner unintelligible to men the "substance" of the bread and wine actually changed into the flesh and blood of Christ, even though the "accidents"—i.e., their outward appearances—remained. That position, known as the doctrine of transubstantiation, has been reaffirmed officially on numerous occasions by Roman Catholic authorities. Some Protestant reformers, including Martin Luther, held to the Catholic view or modifications of it, while the Protestant leader Zwingli, on the other hand, affirmed that the Eucharist is primarily a symbolic memorial and that no transformations in the bread and wine actually occur.

Latter-day Saints, while respecting those who believe in transubstantiation, reject the doctrine. We hold to the view that the sacrament of the Lord's Supper is done in *remembrance* of the body and blood of Christ. The elements (bread and water) are purely symbolic of His sacrifice. Significantly, Latter-day Saints partaking of the sacrament reaffirm their commitment to God the Eternal Father that "they are willing to take upon them the name of [His] son, and always remember him and keep his commandments which he has given them; that they may always have his Spirit to be with them" (D&C 20:77, 79). The same pattern, indeed the identical words, were used in the sacramental prayers of the Nephite church of Jesus Christ (see Mormon 4–5).

The Latter-day Saint view that the sacramental prayers are to be given verbatim, with no deviations in wording by the

priesthood holder administering the sacrament, differs from the
practice of the third-century church. Hippolytus, an important
third-century theologian, did not feel it necessary for the cele-
brant (officiator) of the Eucharist to adhere rigidly to a form of
words: "It is not at all necessary for the bishop in giving thanks to
recite the same words as we have given as if they were to be learnt
by heart. But let each pray according to his capacity. If he can
pray in a long and solemn prayer, it is good. But if in his prayer
he prays at modest length, no one may prevent him, provided
only that his prayer is orthodox."[23]

Granted that the current form of the Roman mass has been
set for centuries, it seems difficult to reconcile the "pray as you
wish" view of Hippolytus with the Latter-day Saint view that a
specified wording be used in the sacramental prayer. If one is
right, the other must be wrong. In my view the opinion of
Hippolytus indicates just how far the third-century church had
strayed from its apostolic moorings.

But it was not only the ordinances that were changed. Over
time every aspect of the liturgy of the church became marked by
"the most advanced ritual spendour," including screening of the
sacrament table with gorgeous curtains, enrichment in the sacramental vessels, elaborate vestments worn by the priests, etc. The
renowned historian Edward Gibbon comments on such develop-
ments as follows:

"The sublime and simple theology of the primitive Christians
was gradually corrupted: and the MONARCHY of heaven, already
clouded by metaphysical subtleties, was degraded by the intro-
duction of a popular mythology which tended to restore the
reign of polytheism.

"As the objects of religion were gradually reduced to the
standard of the imagination, the rites and ceremonies were introduced that seemed most powerfully to affect the sense of the
vulgar. If, in the beginning of the fifth century, Tertullian or

Lactantius [early Christian Fathers], had been suddenly raised from the dead, to assist at the festival of some popular saint or martyr, they would have gazed with astonishment and indignation on the profane spectacle which had succeeded to the pure and spiritual worship of a Christian congregation. As soon as the doors of the church were thrown open, they must have been offended by the smoke of incense, the perfume of flowers, and the glare of lamps and tapers, which diffused, at noon-day, a gaudy, superfluous, and, in their opinion a sacrilegious light. If they approached the balustrade of the altar, they made their way through the prostrate crowd, consisting, for the most part, of strangers and pilgrims, who resorted to the city on the vigil of the feast; and who already felt the strong intoxication of fanaticism, and, perhaps, of wine. Their devout kisses were imprinted on the walls and pavement of the sacred edifice; and their fervent prayers were directed, whatever might be the language of their church, to the bones, the blood, or the ashes of the saint, which were usually concealed, by a linen or silken veil, from the eyes of the vulgar. The Christians frequented the tombs of the martyrs, in the hope of obtaining, from their powerful intercession, every sort of spiritual, but more especially of temporal, blessings. . . . The same uniform original spirit of superstition might suggest, in the most distant ages and countries, the same methods of deceiving the credulity, and of affecting the senses of mankind: but it must ingenuously be confessed that the ministers of the catholic church imitated the profane model which they were impatient to destroy. The most respectable bishops had persuaded themselves that the ignorant rustics would more cheerfully renounce the superstitions of Paganism, if they found some resemblance, some compensation, in the bosom of Christianity. The religion of Constantine achieved, in less than a century, the final conquest of the Roman Empire: but the victors themselves were insensibly subdued by the arts of their vanquished rivals."[24]

If priesthood authority was lost by the early church, as it assuredly was, and if that loss dealt the infant church a fatal blow, as it did, when did the insult occur? We don't know precisely, but the fact that the scriptural and historical record goes completely dark for the better part of a century after about A.D. 90–100 suggests the damage was done early on.

One of the most serious errors into which the church fell was that the scriptures became corrupted. Let us now examine that calamitous series of events.

NOTES

1. *History of the Church*, 6:363.

2. *History of the Church*, 6:478–79.

3. Eusebius, *The History of the Church, from Christ to Constantine*, 96.

4. Phillips, *The Young Church in Action*, 11, 20–21; emphasis in original.

5. *History of the Church*, 3:386.

6. Hinckley, "Priesthood Restoration," 71, 72.

7. Lee, in Conference Report, April 1953, 27. See also D&C 107:8–9, 22, 65–67, 91–92; *History of the Church*, 2:200.

8. Chadwick, *The Early Church*, 41.

9. "St. Ignatius's Epistle to the Trallians," in *The Apostolic Fathers*, 2:92; emphasis added. Tralles was a city on the River Maeander, in Asia Minor.

10. See *The Oxford Dictionary of the Christian Church*, s.v. "Apostolic Succession," 74.

11. Hegesippus was a second-century Jewish-Christian who wrote five books directed against the Gnostics. Though these now survive only in fragments, they are said to have existed in their entirety until the sixteenth or seventeenth century.

12. See Frend, *The Rise of Christianity*, 146.

13. See ibid., 130.

14. See chapter 8 of this book.

15. Tuchman, *The March of Folly*, 52.

16. Manchester, *A World Lit Only by Fire*, 74–86. See also Norwich, *A Short History of Byzantium*, 182. This is a shortened version of Lord Norwich's great trilogy on Byzantine history.

17. Mosheim, *An Ecclesiastical History, Ancient and Modern,* 1:84.

18. *The Didache,* a short early church manual, dating from the late first or early second century A.D., contains instructions on baptism, fasting, prayer, the sacrament and other aspects of early Christian liturgy. The only complete manuscript dates from the eleventh century, and may be corrupted in its content.

19. Augustine (354–430 A.D.), intellectually brilliant bishop of Hippo in North Africa, is revered by many Christians as one of the "Doctors of the Church." He was a Manichean for nine years before embracing Christianity. He contended against Manicheism, Donatism, and Pelagianism. Augustine propounded the doctrine of original sin—that mankind suffers from an inherited moral disease which can be cured only through the grace of God. His most celebrated works are his "Confessions," and the "City of God." He has had an immense influence on Western theological thought from his time until the present. He is revered as a Saint in the Catholic Church.

20. *The Eerdmans Bible Dictionary,* s.v. "Baptism," 123–24.

21. *Encyclopedia of Early Christianity,* s.v. "Baptism," 131–34.

22. This was one of a series of councils held at the Lateran Palace at Rome from the seventh to the eighteenth centuries.

23. Chadwick, *Early Church,* 263.

24. Gibbon, *The History of the Decline and Fall of the Roman Empire,* 3:354–56.

CHAPTER FOUR

CORRUPTION OF THE
SCRIPTURES

IN THE ABSENCE OF APOSTOLIC AUTHORITY, with no one on earth who could say with divine approval, "Thus saith the Lord . . . ," the written word of God took on added importance. Scripture became the only authority remaining to shape the doctrines and chart the future direction of the church. Unfortunately, in the process of translation, interpretation, and preservation, many scriptures were altered, lost, or simply misunderstood. Other texts were forged by various proponents, who purported them to be the authentic works of one apostle or another.

Professor Bart Ehrman, an eminent religious historian who is not a Latter-day Saint, has noted that the scriptural texts we now have are *not* the originals, none of which has survived the passage of time. What we have are "copies made over the course of centuries, or more accurately, copies of the copies of the copies, some 5,366 of these in the Greek language alone, that date from the second century down to the sixteenth. Strikingly, with the exception of the smallest fragments, no two of these copies are exactly alike in all their particulars. No one knows how many

differences, or variant readings, occur among the surviving wit-
nesses, but they must number in the hundreds of thousands."[1]

Hundreds of thousands of changes in the scriptures! Most of
those changes are readily seen to be purely accidental, resulting
from the carelessness, ineptitude, or fatigue of the scribe. The
texts were, after all, written by men of flesh and blood, often
working under less than perfect conditions, subject to the controversies, conflicts, and hardships of their day. Changes that are
obviously accidental include misspellings and the inadvertent
omission or duplication of a word or a line.

But, notes Professor Ehrman, other changes made in the second and third centuries, by both "orthodox" and "heretical"
scribes, were intentional and deliberate, intended to *say* in the
printed text what the scribe thought he *knew* the passage meant,
or should mean. [2] Ehrman contends that these changes were
intended to defend a theological position, while denigrating
those of opponents.[3] Thus, "orthodox" scribes felt compelled to
defend the "orthodox" position that Jesus Christ was the Son of
God, at once both mortal and divine, against charges that He was
not divine, but a mere man (taught by the Ebionites[4]); or that
He was two beings, the mortal Jesus and the divine Christ
(averred by the Valentinian Gnostics[5]). While admitting it is
impossible to determine exactly what scribal intentions were,
Ehrman has uncovered no evidence that "orthodox" scribes of
the second and third centuries acted out of sheer malice, or that
they changed a text to say what they knew it did not.[6] They made
changes, he believes, to make sure *their* understanding of what a
text meant was absolutely clear to any reader. And it is the
"orthodox" rather than "heretical" versions that have survived.
Ehrman notes, wryly, "that the winners not only write the
history, they also reproduce the texts." [7]

Ehrman's claim of the absence of malice on the part of
"orthodox" scribes must be measured against the Nephite

account that those who "have taken away from the gospel of the Lamb many parts which are plain and most precious" (1 Nephi 13:26) did so that "they might pervert the right ways of the Lord, that they might blind the eyes and harden the hearts of the children of men" (1 Nephi 13:27). Someone, or more likely a group of people, whether "orthodox" or "heretical," made scriptural changes with malice aforethought, deliberately seeking to pervert the truth and advance a false cause. I am convinced both "orthodox" and "heretical" scribes must share the blame. "Heretical" teachings about the nature of Christ probably did most of their damage early on, drawing many people away from the truth in the first few centuries A.D., while the texts were not yet canonized,[8] but "orthodox" teachings, as exemplified in the Nicene Creed, also are replete with error and confusion.

It seems certain that the changes that most significantly corrupted the scriptures came early in the Christian era. Professor John Gee of Brigham Young University is of the view that "we neither need to nor should look later than the second century for these changes."[9] There are, indeed, many allegations by second-century Christian writers that others were corrupting the scriptures. Tertullian, the first Christian Father who wrote in Latin, and who lived and worked during the last half of the second and early third centuries, wrote extensively about a number of heretic Christian sects, including that of Marcion. Marcion, a gifted organizer and charismatic leader, rejected almost all Christian scriptures, accepting only Paul's epistles and an edited version of Luke (see chapter 8). He and his followers introduced dramatic elements of doctrinal error into the Church in the latter half of the second century. Of Marcion, Tertullian wrote, "[He] expressly and openly used the knife, not the pen, since he made such an excision of the Scriptures as suited his own subject matter."[10] Marcion, wrote Tertullian, "mutilated the Gospel according to Luke, removing all the narratives of the Lord's birth, and also removing much of the teaching of the discourses of the Lord."[11]

Irenaeus, the bishop of Lyons at the end of the second century A.D., claimed that a sect, the followers of Valentinus (perhaps the most influential of the Gnostics) changed the scriptures "by transferring passages, and dressing them up anew, and making one thing out of another."[12] Clement of Alexandria (A.D. 150–215), the teacher of Origen, and a professor at Alexandria, a man thoroughly infused with Greek philosophy, railed similarly against the Carpocratians, another Gnostic sect. Charges of deliberate falsification of the scriptures flew thick and fast. Dionysius, bishop of Corinth in the late second century, complained that his own epistles had been tampered with, and added ruefully, "Small wonder then if some have dared to tamper even with the word of the Lord Himself, when they have conspired to mutilate my own humble efforts."[13]

Without going into more detail, it is clear that allegations of scriptural tampering and downright forgery were rampant in the second century of the Christian era. No individual or group was immune; not only were heretical sects like the Gnostics implicated, but so also was the group that eventually morphed into "orthodox" Christianity.

How then could the corruption have proceeded? What methods would have been used? They include the following:

1. *Misinterpretation and subsequent wresting of the scriptures.* Peter seems to be alluding to this occurring even in his time: "And account that the longsuffering of our Lord is salvation; even as our beloved brother Paul also according to the wisdom given unto him hath written unto you; as also in all his epistles, speaking in them of these things; in which are some things hard to be understood, which they that are unlearned and unstable

wrest, as they do also the other scriptures, unto their own destruction" (2 Peter 3:15–16).

To wrest the scriptures for private interpretation is one thing: to do so for public transmission of aberrant views is even more serious. Those who carry out either distortion "have gone far astray," as Alma said to his son Corianton. Contention and wresting the scriptures go hand in hand, as the Lord explained to Joseph Smith:

"I am he who said—Other sheep have I which are not of this fold—unto my disciples, and many there were that understood me not.

"And I will show unto this people that I had other sheep, and that they were a branch of the house of Jacob;

"And I will bring to light their marvelous works, which they did in my name;

"Yea, and I will also bring to light my gospel which was ministered unto them, and, behold, they shall not deny that which you have received, but they shall build it up, and shall bring to light the true points of my doctrine, yea, and the only doctrine which is in me.

"And this I do that I may establish my gospel, that there may not be so much contention; yea, Satan doth stir up the hearts of the people to contention concerning the points of my doctrine; and in these things they do err, for they do wrest the scriptures and do not understand them" (D&C 10:59–63).

As noted previously, the problem of misinterpretation and subsequent distortion (i.e., wresting) of the scriptures was perhaps most acute in the young church where not much was yet written down.

Reinterpretation of the scriptures, to consider them in an allegorical framework, rather than as literal truths, was another common fault amongst early Christian writers. It was a manifestation of the internal corrosion that was a real threat to the church and, at least by the third century, of the effects of Greek philosophy on Christian doctrines. Such wresting of the scriptures leads inevitably to the rise of men "speaking perverse things, to draw away disciples after them" (Acts 20:30).

Yet another way to reinterpret scriptural texts is to change the meaning of the words. Professor Gee points out that this topic has not received the treatment it deserves, but he notes that an example would be the change in the word *mysterion* from "(initiation) rite" to "secret."[14]

2. *Deletion of words or ideas.* This is the fault ascribed by Tertullian to Marcion, mentioned above.

3. *False attribution of text.* Tertullian discusses forged documents, falsely attributed to Paul, which circulated in his day.[15] That brings up the whole topic of the authorship of the books of the New Testament. Scholars, as usual, are divided. Some dispute the authorship of various books attributed to Paul, including Hebrews and the Pastoral Letters; others dispute the authorship of 2 Peter, Jude, two of John's epistles, Ephesians, even John's gospel and Revelation, among others.

WHY WERE THE TEXTS CORRUPTED?

It is impossible, after two millennia, to be very definitive about motivation. We can only guess at why those who deliberately and maliciously corrupted the scriptures did so. But the old sins of pride, rebellion, usurpation of authority, the love of power, all the self-inflicted wounds that tore apart the church in Corinth, for example, must be high on any list. So too must attempts to cover up sin, whether it be idolatry, sexual licentiousness, the love of worldly things. In the vision he was granted, Nephi enumerated the characteristics of the great and abominable church: "And the angel spake unto me, saying: Behold the gold, and the silver, and the silks, and the scarlets, and the fine-twined linen, and precious clothing, and the harlots, [these] are the desires of this great and abominable church" (1 Nephi 13:8).

Finally, there are the attempts by heretics—the Gnostics, in all their manifestations; the Marcionites; the Manicheans, to name but three especially troublesome sects. They corrupted the scriptures in order to seduce people away from viewpoints other than their own, to embellish their claims to validity while deprecating those of their opponents, and to set themselves up, therefore, as the legitimate heirs of the apostles. It must be admitted, however, that those Christians who later became the "orthodox" group were not themselves averse to changing facts to meet their perceived needs.

The Gnostics were particularly adept at professing beliefs held by other Christians, on the surface at least, while ascribing to them mystical meanings. Their tactics drove many orthodox leaders to distraction. Authorities such as Irenaeus found the Gnostic interpretations to be both absurd and contradicted by the "clear and plain" teachings of scripture. To Irenaeus, the Gnostic use of scripture was comparable to a person who, "observing a beautiful mosaic of a king, decides to dismantle the precious stones and reassemble them in the likeness of a mongrel dog, claiming that this was what the artist intended all along."[16]

Some Christians, while perhaps grudgingly admitting that scriptural copyists made accidental mistakes, reject the idea there have been substantive and deliberate changes in the Biblical scriptures from the first writing to the present. But that argument carries no weight, if the corruption occurred during the first two centuries of the Christian era. There simply are no manuscripts of biblical scripture available to us that date from the first century; only a tiny fragment containing but ten complete words of the New Testament book of John (the Rylands Fragment; see chapter 1) dates from the second century. There is nothing else from the period when it is probable the most serious damage to the scriptures was being done. Most of the copies of the Pauline Epistles available to us, and substantial parts of the Gospels, Acts, Isaiah, Ezekiel, Daniel, and Esther date from the early third century at the earliest.

Vellum[17] uncials (written in majuscule script) were commissioned by the Emperor Constantine in the fourth century. Eusebius recorded the emperor's command: "I have thought it expedient to instruct your Intelligence [Constantine here directs Eusebius] that you should command to be written fifty volumes on prepared vellum, easy to read and conveniently portable, by professional scribes with an exact understanding of their craft—volumes, that is to say, of the Holy Scriptures, the provision and use of which is, as you are aware, most necessary for the instruction of the Church. Letters have been dispatched from our Clemency [i.e., Constantine] to the accountant of the province, advising him to supply everything requisite for the production of the books, and it will be your care to ensure that they are prepared as quickly as possible. Using the authority of this letter you should commandeer two public carriages for their transport, for by such means will these fine volumes be most readily brought before our eyes, this duty being performed by one of the deacons of your church, who on reaching our presence will experience our liberality."[18]

Only an emperor could have issued such an order: production of fifty Bibles would have required the skins of 4,500 calves. It cannot be proven, but it is probable, at least so some experts assert, that the famous *Codex Sinaiticus* was one of the fifty copies commissioned by Constantine. It was found by a German professor in a monastery on Mount Sinai in 1859. Sold originally to the Russian czar, most of the *Codex* now is held by the British Library. *Sinaiticus* contains the Old Testament as we know it, and the New Testament, with the addition of the Epistle of Barnabas and part of the Shepherd of Hermas (the latter two books are not found in the King James Bible).

We simply do not have scriptural material from the beginning of the second century to compare with that at the end of that century, by which time damage to the scriptures largely had been done. But Christian writers of the late first century, such as Clement of Rome,[19] quote numerous scriptural passages that are not found in our current Bible. Even quotations made from scriptures in our current Bible are not the same as those we now have. We cannot avoid the conclusion that the scriptures, as Nephi indicated, have indeed been "kept back"—that is, corrupted, deleted, or added to. But the proof, in any empirical sense, simply is not available. The early manuscripts are gone, forever, I fear.

Of course, it is possible that a great cache of previously unknown New Testament manuscripts, of very early origin, may be found somewhere. But that seems increasingly unlikely. We should not give up hope, however. After all, the Book of Thomas, an apocryphal Gnostic work cited by Origen[20] in the third century, was discovered in Egypt in 1945. And the Dead Sea Scrolls, found between 1947 and 1956, and probably dating from about 20 B.C. to A.D. 70, are providing valuable information on early Old Testament and other texts. Additionally, there are many papyrus rolls in the hands of museums, universities, etc., awaiting translation. Most, undoubtedly, deal with mundane things—commercial transactions and the like—but it is at least possible one or more of them contains valuable religious material, previously unknown to the modern world.

THE ROLE OF THE GREAT AND ABOMINABLE CHURCH

The Nephite record testifies of the nefarious role of a "great and abominable church" in taking away many plain and precious

things from the sacred scripture (see 1 Nephi 13:26). Professor
Stephen E. Robinson has discussed the nature of the "great and
abominable church," the spiritual Babylon, which wars against
the Saints of God. It is the church of the devil, the "whore of all
the earth" (2 Nephi 10:16), which "seeks the lusts of the flesh
and all the things of the world" (1 Nephi 22:23). Professor
Robinson points out that the "great and abominable church" is
"an immense assembly or association of people bound together
by their loyalty to that which God hates. Most likely this 'church'
is involved specifically in sexual immorality, idolatry (that is, false
worship), or both." [21] The great and abominable church did its
dirty work after the Jews had transmitted the Bible in its purity
to the Gentiles (see 1 Nephi 13:24–26). Furthermore, its dark-
est deeds probably occurred right after the apostles had "fallen
asleep"—i.e., by the end of the first century (see D&C 86:3). But
make no mistake, its work was under way in the first century. One
of the most significant ways by which the "great and abominable
church" corrupted the scriptures was to "keep back" plain and
precious parts of the gospel of the Lamb, such that important
truths were lost (see 1 Nephi 13:32–34).

Historically, what could be the identity of the "great and
abominable church," which corrupted the scriptures? Could it
have been the Jews? It seems highly unlikely. Though the Jews
and Christians squabbled and fought often during the first three
centuries of the Christian era, it simply does not make sense that
the Jews, whose record was taken forth "in purity unto the
Gentiles," (1 Nephi 13:25) would tamper with their own record.
Furthermore, to even suggest that Judaism has the odious characteristics of the "great and abominable church" is to indulge in
the foulest of calumnies against a great people who have been
maligned and persecuted by far too many, Christians included.
Well, then, what about the Roman Catholic or Eastern Orthodox
churches? Even though these churches have been guilty of many

errors over the centuries, the answer must again be a most emphatic "no." The Roman Catholic church, as we know it, didn't even exist in the first two centuries of the Christian era, when the "great and abominable church" was especially active in corrupting the scriptures. Even if we consider as Catholic (i.e., universal) the church Constantine sponsored early in the fourth century A.D. as part of a larger strategy to bring unity to his troubled empire, it is plain that the changes to the scripture had long since been perpetrated. The church was, by then, already apostate. The injury was already done, long before the "universal" church can be identified as such.

In passing, let us also lay to rest the not uncommon misperception that the scriptures were corrupted by malicious medieval monks. During the long centuries before the invention of printing in the fourteenth century A.D., in the days (beginning in about the sixth century A.D.) when the Bible was copied by hand in monasteries throughout Europe, mistakes certainly were made by the copyists, as already noted. But those mistakes were, in general at least, accidents, the results of carelessness or ineptitude, often the fallout, one imagines, from working long hours in cold and fatigue, bent over vellum pages, in the *scriptorium*[22] of a monastery. We actually owe a great debt to those anonymous copyists, who preserved the Bible for subsequent generations, and in the process helped ensure the continuance of Christian culture.

We cannot clearly identify the leaders and members of the "great and abominable church," though we understand much of its nature. But that does not mean it was not real. It still exists. Its members are bound by one great loyalty—to Satan and his devilish work. As Stephen Robinson has said: "Membership [in the great and abominable church] is based more on who has your heart than on who has your records."[23] By that reasoning, as Robinson has noted, there undoubtedly are people who call themselves Latter-day Saints who belong to the "great and abominable church," and members of other churches who do not, because they strive to follow the Lamb of God and aspire to become like Him.

It is most probable, I believe, that the great and abominable church, which maliciously corrupted the scriptures early in the Christian era, was actually not a single entity, but a coalition, or at least a conglomerate, of people who rebelled against God. Those who called themselves Christian but rebelled against the leaders and quarreled with their fellows, who practiced idolatry, who wallowed in mysticism, who couldn't fully leave Judaism, who betrayed other Christians, who responded to persecution by craven recanting of their testimony of Christ—those and others like them ensured that the infant church would receive a fatal blow, such that the "mystery of iniquity" would prevail. The deliberate corrupters of the scriptures surely are found among this motley crew.

DISPUTES OVER THE CANON OF SCRIPTURE

At the beginning of the Christian era, there obviously were no written scriptures. The gospel message initially was transmitted orally, first by Jesus and later by the apostles and their associates. The authors of early Christian writings probably were little interested in contributing to a future canon of doctrinally "acceptable" books. In the main, their writings were intended to tell the "good news" about Jesus, to proclaim His role as redeeming Savior, and to strengthen, edify, and educate new and struggling Christian communities throughout the Roman empire. But by the middle of the second century, it is believed that written Gospels, and other sayings attributed to Jesus, began to circulate among Christians, and to be used in their meetings. It must be noted, however, that the earliest portions of the materials in the Chester Beatty papyri,[24] which contains substantial portions of several Old and New Testament books, plus the last eleven chapters of the Book of Enoch (not included in the current King James version of the Bible), date from the third century A.D.

In a sense, the current Christian canon owes its existence to Marcion, a mid–second-century bishop's son, and a heretic who denied any Jewish connections with Jesus and the Old Testament (see chapter 8). Marcion produced a list of what he considered the authentic writings of the Christian faith. It included some but not all of Paul's letters, and a revision of Luke's gospel, which carefully excludes all mention of the Jews. Orthodoxy began to be defined, in part, by listing the sacred texts "acceptable" to Christians, and excluding all others, including those of heretical sects.

But what books should be contained in the canon of scripture? About A.D. 170 (or perhaps in the fourth century; scholars are in dispute on the matter), someone in Rome wrote, in Greek, a list of books considered canonical by the Roman church at that time. It constitutes the earliest record of canonical books available to us. A portion (70 lines) of this list, called the Muratorian Canon,[25] was found in the Ambrosian library in Milan in 1740, by a man named Lodovico Muratori. It was written in very rough Latin, by someone who probably copied it from the Greek in the eighth century. The Muratorian Canon lists the four Gospels, and the other books in the New Testament except Hebrews, James, and 1 and 2 Peter, but also includes two other books not in the current New Testament canon: the Apocalypse of Peter, and the Wisdom of Solomon. It rejects the Shepherd of Hermas, the Marcionite epistles of Paul to Laodicia and Alexandria, and a series of other Gnostic and other "heretical" writings. The Marcionite epistles mentioned are clear and obvious forgeries.

Hermas was not a forgery and presented what was considered "orthodox" doctrine, but was not apostolic in origin.

Eusebius,[26] writing about A.D. 300, differentiated between generally accepted books, those of uncertain status, and books that definitely should be excluded from the canon of scripture. Hebrews, James, 2 Peter, 2 and 3 John, Jude, and Revelation were considered by Eusebius to be questionable. Agreement on the contents of the New Testament canon, insofar as the Eastern church was concerned, developed after Athanasius, the metropolitan (bishop) of Alexandria, recommended a canonical list in A.D. 367 in a letter he wrote to church members in North Africa, over whom he had jurisdiction. (We will learn much more about Athanasius in chapter 6.) This list contained all of the books of the present New Testament. A papal decree of A.D. 403 confirmed the canon of Athanasius for use in the Western church, but the canon of scripture was not finally set authoritatively for Roman Catholics until the Council of Trent in the sixteenth century.

Some churches, notably the Syrian Orthodox and Chaldean Syrian, continue to reject 2 Peter, 2 and 3 John, Jude, and the book of Revelation. The Greek Orthodox church has never included the book of Revelation. At the other extreme, the Ethiopian church includes, to our day, 38 books in its official list of New Testament scriptures. In addition to the 27 books accepted as canonical by most other churches, the Ethiopian church includes the Shepherd of Hermas, two epistles of Clement, and a collection of ecclesiastical law called the Apostolic Constitutions.

The Latin version of the Bible most widely used in the West for a thousand years was the Vulgate, translated by Jerome[27] at the command of Pope Damasus in the late fourth or early fifth centuries. It contains, in addition to the books in the King James version, twelve others—Tobit, Judith, the Wisdom of Solomon,

Ecclesiastes or Ben Sirech, Baruch, the Letter of Jeremiah, 1 and 2 Maccabees, and additions to Daniel. These twelve had been in the Greek translation of the Old Testament, the Septuagint, used by the early Christian church, and passed therefrom to the Vulgate of the Roman church.

Margaret Barker, a noted British scholar, blames Jerome for giving up the more accurate and complete version of scriptures found in the Greek Old Testament in favor of the version used by Hellenized Jews. Evidence that the early Christian church quoted from Old Testament scriptures no longer known to us indicates either that early Christians used different versions of books in the current Hebrew canon, or that they had access to books other than those that eventually became part of the Hebrew canon—for example, the book of 1 Enoch. Incidentally, the writings now known as 1 Enoch were lost to Western Christianity until rediscovered in Ethiopia in 1770. First Enoch had, however, been available in Constantinople, and hence to Eastern Christians, at the end of the eighth century. The book of 2 Enoch evidently traveled with Christian missionaries when they brought the gospel to Russia, since it is found in the Old Slavonic language.[28]

The Protestant reformation introduced other challenges. Martin Luther believed that Hebrews, James, Jude, and Revelation did not belong among the "true and noblest" books of the New Testament. Some Protestants termed these books apocryphal, and they were so considered by certain Protestants for nearly a century.

The point of this brief summary simply is that there is no universally agreed upon canon of New Testament scripture, and there never has been one. But most Christians, by the fifth century A.D., believed the canon of scripture was closed. Bereft of apostolic direction and the revelation which underlies it, the church had reached the erroneous conclusion that God had said all He ever intended to say, for all time. The canon of scripture was closed and complete. The heavens were shut. Is it any wonder that "orthodox" Christianity shuddered when the Book of Mormon, another testament of Jesus Christ, was translated and given to the world?

NOTES

1. Ehrman, *The Orthodox Corruption of Scripture*, 27.
2. See ibid., 276.
3. Ibid., 275.
4. See chapter 8 of this book.
5. Ibid.
6. See Ehrman, *Orthodox Corruption of Scripture*, 280.
7. Ibid., 27.
8. See ibid., 277.
9. Gee, "The Corruption of Scripture in the Second Century," 1.
10. Tertullian, *On Prescription Against Heretics*, in *The Ante-Nicean Fathers*, 3:262.
11. *Documents of the Christian Church*, 37.
12. Irenaeus, *Contra Haereses*, in *The Ante-Nicean Fathers*, 1:326.
13. Eusebius, *The History of the Church from Christ to Constantine*, 132.
14. Gee, "The Corruption of Scripture in the Second Century," 10.
15. See Tertullian, in *The Ante-Nicean Fathers*, 3:677.
16. Ehrman, *The Orthodox Corruption of Scripture*, 21.
17. Vellum is fine-grained unsplit lambskin, kidskin, or calfskin prepared especially as writing material.
18. Quoted in Romer, *Testament*, 226.
19. Clement of Rome was supposedly bishop of Rome, the third after Peter, although neither assertion can be proven. He may have been the Clement mentioned by Paul in Philippians 4:3. His first epistle (Clement I) was written about A.D. 96 in the name of the church at Rome, to deal with strife in the church at Corinth.
20. Origen (circa A.D. 185–254), a brilliant and prolific scholar, was born in Egypt, probably in Alexandria. His father was martyred in A.D. 202 and Origen escaped a similar fate only because of his mother's assistance. He was thoroughly trained in philosophy and literature. Most of his extensive writings on theological matters have been lost and a satisfactory

reconstruction of his thoughts is not always possible. His teachings were much influenced by Greek philosophy.

21. Robinson, "Warring Against the Saints of God," 34–35.

22. The scriptorium was the workroom in a monastery where copies of the scriptures were handwritten by scribes.

23. Robinson, "Warring Against the Saints of God," 37.

24. The Chester Beatty papyri are a group of manuscripts found in Egypt, and acquired by Mr. Chester Beatty in 1931. All are incomplete, but several are of substantial size. They include parts of the books of Genesis, Numbers, Deuteronomy, Ecclesiastes, Isaiah, Jeremiah, Ezekiel, Daniel, Esther, the Gospels, Acts, the Pauline epistles, and Revelation. Eleven chapters of the apocryphal Book of Enoch also are included. Most of the manuscripts are of third- and fourth-century origin, a century or more older than the earliest known vellum manuscript.

25. See *Documents of the Christian Church*, 28–29.

26. Eusebius (circa A.D. 260–340) was bishop of Caesarea, and is known as the "Father of Church History." His most famous writing is his *Ecclesiastical History*, in ten volumes, giving valuable information on the history of Christianity from the apostolic period to the fourth century. His *Life of Constantine* is a flattering portrayal of the Roman Emperor.

27. Jerome (circa A.D. 342–420) was at one time a hermit, but later served as secretary to Pope Damasus. He translated the Bible into Latin from the original languages, and is now revered as a Catholic Saint.

28. See Barker, *The Great High Priest*, 301.

CHAPTER FIVE

PERSECUTION AND MARTYRDOM

Sometime late in the year A.D. 112, the governor of the Roman province of Bithynia-Pontus wrote a letter to his superior, the Emperor Trajan. The nephew and adopted son of an aristocratic Roman citizen of the senatorial class, the governor was known as Pliny the Younger, to distinguish him from his famous kinsman, Pliny the Elder, who died in A.D. 79 in the flame and ash of the eruption of Mount Vesuvius.[1] Pliny the Younger had risen steadily through the ranks of the civil bureaucracy of Rome, culminating in his appointment (well deserved in Pliny's view) as governor of an important part of the empire. Well educated, an experienced and able administrator, sound of judgment, and conservative by temperament, Pliny could be counted on to represent his emperor with diligence and prudence.

Pliny had received complaints from local citizens, probably merchants and other businesspeople, about a group called Christians. Among the complainers may have been butchers, upset because of reduced sales of meats used to make sacrifices to the emperor and the "immortal gods" of Rome.

In most parts of the Roman empire Christians at that time

87

were of little concern to the civil authorities. Local magistrates
were inclined to bring charges or initiate legal actions against
Christians only if complaints were received. Complaints varied
from the intensely personal—domestic quarrels between
Christian and non-Christian spouses, a neighbor's envy or jeal-
ousy over a Christian's wealth or better job, and so on—to the
more generic, relating to the Christians' perceived lack of respect
for the "immortal gods," as evidenced by their "obstinate"
refusals to make sacrifices to them. Such "atheism," in Roman
eyes, simply begged for retribution by the gods themselves, who
would, it was feared, vent their anger on the whole community
in the form of famine, plague, drought, or war.

For much of the first four centuries of the Christian era, few
of those in charge, from local magistrate to governor, cared one
way or the other what Christians did or did not believe. A simple
gesture of honor to the gods and conformity to long-established
tradition were all that was required. Whether such was sincere or
not wasn't the issue. Roman religion was never a matter of
devoutness. It dealt only with ritual. But religion could not be
separated from the state. To attack or fail to defend the one was
to damage the other. In a great number of instances over the
years the authorities bent over backwards to persuade Christians
to "get over" their perceived obstinacy and un-Roman behavior.
The authorities wanted worshipers of the old gods of Rome, or
at least a sensible acknowledgment of them, not martyrs for a
faith. Of course, some local authorities also may have feared that
failure to take action against Christians might disturb the peace
in their locale, and that word would get back to their superiors,
who might criticize their lack of zeal.

And there were recurrent, largely unfounded rumors of
Christian immorality, especially in the early years. But opposition
to Christians had little of religious zeal to it.

But back to Pliny and his letter to Trajan. Pliny, though not totally unfamiliar with Christians, apparently had only slight and largely secondhand information about them. He knew that on previous occasions, some of them in the distant past, Roman authorities had been required to deal with troublesome foreign groups. The Roman historian Livy, writing more than a century before Pliny's time, recounts how the Roman senate in 186 B.C. had suppressed the Bacchic cult—a Grecian group that indulged in drunken orgies in the forests. Pliny may have feared, without any firm evidence, that the Christians were guilty of similar undesirable practices.

Pliny's letter to Trajan follows:

"It is my rule, Sire, to refer to you in matters where I am uncertain. For who can better direct my hesitation or instruct my ignorance? I was never present at any trial of Christians; therefore I do not know what are the customary penalties or investigations, and what limits are observed. I have hesitated a great deal on the question whether there should be any distinction of ages; whether the weak should have the same treatment as the more robust; whether those who recant should be pardoned, or whether a man who has ever been a Christian should gain nothing by ceasing to be such; whether the name itself, even if innocent of crime, should be punished, or only the crimes attaching to that name.

"Meanwhile, this is the course that I have adopted in the case of those brought before me as Christians. I ask them if they are Christians. If they admit it I repeat the question a second and a third time, threatening capital punishment; if they persist I sentence them to death. For I do not doubt that, whatever kind of crime it may be to which they have confessed, their pertinacity and inflexible obstinacy should certainly be punished. There were others who displayed a like madness and whom I reserved to be sent to Rome, since they were Roman citizens.

"Thereupon the usual result followed; the very fact of my

dealing with the question led to a wider spread of the charge, and a great variety of cases were brought before me. An anonymous pamphlet was issued, containing many names. All who denied that they were or had been Christians I considered should be discharged, because they called upon the gods at my dictation and did reverence, with incense and wine, to your image which I had ordered to be brought forward for this purpose, together with the statues of the deities; and especially because they cursed Christ, a thing which, it is said, genuine Christians cannot be induced to do. Others named by the informer first said that they were Christians and then denied it; declaring that they had been but were so no longer, some having recanted three years or more before and one or two as long ago as twenty years. They all worshipped your image and the statues of the gods and cursed Christ. But they declared that the sum of their guilt or error had amounted only to this, that on an appointed day they had been accustomed to meet before daybreak, and to recite a hymn antiphonally to Christ, as to a god, and to bind themselves by an oath, not for the commission of any crime but to abstain from theft, robbery, adultery and breach of faith, and not to deny a deposit when it was claimed. After the conclusion of this ceremony it was their custom to depart and meet again to take food; but it was ordinary and harmless food, and they had ceased this practice after my edict in which, in accordance with your orders, I had forbidden secret societies. I thought it the more necessary, therefore, to find out what truth there was in this by applying torture to two maidservants, who were called deaconesses. But I found nothing but a depraved and extravagant superstition, and I therefore postponed my examination and had recourse to you for consultation.

"The matter seemed to me to justify my consulting you, especially on account of the number of those imperilled; for many persons of all ages and classes and of both sexes are being put in peril by accusation, and this will go on. The contagion of this superstition has spread not only in the cities, but in the villages and rural districts as well; yet it seems capable of being checked and set right. There is no shadow of doubt that the temples, which have been almost deserted, are beginning to be frequented once more, that the sacred rites which have been long neglected are being renewed, and that sacrificial victims are for sale everywhere, whereas, till recently, a buyer was rarely to be found. From this it is easy to imagine what a host of men could be set right, were they given a chance to recantation."[2]

Note Pliny's reference to his discovery that Christians, in their ceremonies, took food, but it was "ordinary and harmless" food. Pliny may well have had in mind scandalous rumors already circulating of monstrous behavior by Christians, who were accused of cannibalism (eating the blood and flesh of their God). Pliny wanted to satisfy himself the rumors were not true. I suspect Pliny's concern was not so much because he cared if the stories *were* true, but rather because if they were *false,* Christians represented less of a threat to the Roman sense of decent and proper behavior. Indeed, after Pliny's letter, it was generally known among the ruling classes, as Robin Lane Fox has pointed out, that "the extreme allegations of Christian vice were false."[3] Such lurid stories remained rife among the general populace for many more years, however, and undoubtedly played a part in shaping public and official attitudes toward Christians.

But it must be said, and it is a mark of the apostasy already ripping out the vitals of the church by the early second century, that apostate groups, calling themselves Christian, *did* indulge in licentious and bizarre rites and practices. A number of early Christian writers, including Clement of Alexandria[4] (early third century A.D.) and Justin Martyr[5] (middle of the second century) implicate various groups, including a Gnostic sect called the Carpocratians, in such activities.

Note also that many who called themselves Christian folded under pressure and turned against God: denying the faith, they "cursed Christ," as Pliny said in his letter to Trajan. Hollywood-inspired myths that all Christians went happily to their deaths rather than denying Christ simply are not true. As in every age, including, sadly, our own, not everyone who joins the church of Jesus Christ remains faithful to the end of mortality.

Trajan's reply to Pliny is short and to the point: "You have taken the right line, my dear Pliny, in examining the cases of those denounced to you as Christians, for no hard and fast rule can be laid down, of universal application. They are not to be sought out; if they are informed against, and the charge is proved, they are to be punished, with this reservation—that if any one denies that he is a Christian, and actually proves it, that is by worshipping our gods, he shall be pardoned as a result of his recantation, however suspect he may have been with respect to the past. Pamphlets published anonymously should carry no weight in any charge whatsoever. They constitute a very bad precedent, and are also out of keeping with this age."[6]

So Trajan supported his governor, while insisting that the Christians be treated fairly and even-handedly. They were not to be subject to malicious slander and anonymous allegations of mis-behavior. "In practice," as W. H. C. Frend points out, "this was toleration, except for victims of popular hatred or private vendetta."[7] Sporadic persecution of Christians, at least on a local scale, had, however, begun several decades before Pliny wrote his famous letter.

In A.D. 64, a disastrous fire gutted entire districts of Rome. For reasons unknown to this day, Nero, the Roman emperor at that time, attempted to make the Christians of Rome the scape-goats. Nero himself was suspected by some of being responsible for the disaster, and he undoubtedly wanted to divert the blame to someone else. Some have claimed that orthodox Jews in the city, afraid *they* might be blamed for the conflagration, may have prompted Nero to take his position. And memories of the Bacchanalian conspiracy more than two centuries before (see page 89) raised concerns about what could happen if foreign cults got out of hand. For whatever reason, Nero, a man noted for his stupidity and cruelty, ordered the most brutal punishments for the Christians of Rome. Christians, reportedly by the hundreds (though that number may be exaggerated) were murdered—some of them soaked in pitch and used as ghastly torches at garden parties. According to the Roman historian Tacitus:[8] "An immense multitude was convicted, not so much on the charge of arson as because of hatred of the human race. Besides being put to death they were made to serve as objects of amusement; they were clad in the hides of beasts and torn to death by dogs; others were crucified, others set on fire to serve to illuminate the night when daylight failed. Nero had thrown open his grounds for the display, and was putting on a show in the circus, where he mingled with the people in the dress of a charioteer or drove about in his chariot. All this gave rise to a feeling of pity, even towards men whose guilt merited the most exemplary punishment; for it was felt that they were being destroyed not for the public good but to gratify the cruelty of an individual."[9]

As noted previously, the Apostles Peter and Paul may have been killed during the Neronian persecution. Christian tradition avers as much, but we simply do not know for sure. It has been suggested that the trial and subsequent execution of Paul may have brought the Christians to Nero's attention, making it easy for him to use them as scapegoats responsible for the great fire.[10] Others are of the view that disgruntled Jewish-Christians, perhaps jealous of successful proselytizing efforts among the "Gentiles," and still clinging to the false belief that Christianity was just a branch of reformed Judaism, may have betrayed the two apostles to the Roman authorities.[11] If that view is correct, and there is no way to prove or disprove it, the belief that the early church was racked with dissension is strengthened significantly.

Some of Nero's persecution of Christians in Rome extended to the provinces as governors took the lead from what was happening at the center of the empire. Recall that Pliny had said in his letter to Trajan, "I have not been present at the trials of Christians," clearly implying that other men of senior rank had been present. It seems apparent, however, that Nero's persecution was both temporary and limited. Fortunately for everyone, not least the Christians, Nero was overthrown and killed four years after the fire in Rome.

There is no need or advantage to even attempt to recount every episode of organized terrorism against the Christians until the Edict of Toleration in A.D. 311. Throughout the years, Christians made convenient scapegoats for whatever tragedy occurred. As Tertullian[12] (A.D. 160–220) noted wryly: "If the Tiber reaches the walls, if the Nile failes to rise to the fields, if the sky doesn't move, or the earth does, if there is famine or plague, the cry is at once: 'The Christians to the Lion!'"[13]

It would, however, seem useful to briefly mention a couple of highlights from the history of long, though intermittent, persecution. In A.D. 94, when Domitian was emperor, Christians in Rome suffered persecution in an event that separated Christians from Jews. Domitian had ordered a tax on Jews, and his agents pursued this goal with relentless ferocity, attempting to establish who were Jews and who merely lived like Jews. Christians were at risk because many were former Jews. If Jewish converts to Christianity denied they were Jews in order to escape the tax, they asserted their Christianity, which was even worse. Many were martyred, according to reports: "Conversion to Christianity, like conversion to Judaism, meant putting oneself outside the ambit of Roman religion. . . . To opt for Christianity was also to opt for a religion that had no claim to acceptance by the standards of antiquity or as a national cult, such as Judaism had."[14]

There is a long-standing Christian tradition, unverifiable of course, that Domitian had the surviving members of Jesus' family sent for. Two grandsons of Jude, the half-brother of Jesus, reportedly were brought to Rome from Judea. After questioning them, Domitian is said to have found them harmless farmers with callused hands, and set them free.[15] Did it happen? We don't know. Tradition is not an infallible reflection of truth. Perhaps it is only a story. But the possibility is intriguing.

The dates on which various men and women had been martyred came to be commemorated each year in Christian meetings. The lives, deaths, and bodily parts of martyrs became objects of veneration. It was not long until the cult of the martyrs was firmly established. A few words of explanation seem warranted.

THE CULT OF THE MARTYRS

Over the years, particularly after periods of active persecution, and certainly by the end of the second century A.D., Christians began to see in the deaths of their fellows as a result of persecution the most desirable of all fates. Stories of martyrs were used both as a memorial to the individual and as a "training" and inspiration for future martyrdom. Martyrs, so an apostate church began to believe, had special favor with God. Their deaths, so it was said, washed away all sin after baptism: pure and spotless, "friends of the Lord," martyrs went straight to heaven, their deaths considered "a Eucharistic offering in which [their] blood was to be the wine and [their bodies], crunched by beasts, the bread of God."[16] Or so it was believed!

Martyrs-in-waiting "lusted" for death. Many of them dreamed of their future deaths and told all who would listen about what, to the martyr-in-training, was a much-anticipated event. Polycarp, the aged bishop of Smyrna who was martyred in A.D. 155, saw in a "trance" his pillow set on fire, and said to his companion, "I must needs be burned alive."[17] Ignatius, bishop of Antioch, traveled in great style en route to Rome where he was martyred circa A.D. 107. On his journey he met with various admiring Christian communities and wrote to influential friends, begging they *not* deprive him of his martyrdom by intervening with the pagan authorities.[18] Martyrs endured almost indescribable agonies during their final ordeals, but supposedly did not suffer, meeting death with joy and serenity. They received near-universal admiration from other Christians. It was not uncommon for lapsed Christians, acutely concerned that their personal unfaithfulness had disqualified them from receiving celestial rewards, to attempt to expiate their guilt by provoking their own arrest, in hopes of being martyred. More commonly, however, "volunteers" for martyrdom came from those (often young men) who with singleness of heart longed for the heavenly rewards and earthly esteem which it was believed came to the martyr.

Martyrs, it came to be believed, served as heavenly intercessors between God and man. Soon a thriving trade arose in obtaining and preserving the body parts of martyrs, even dust from the martyr's tomb, which were credited with supernatural powers of healing and blessing and venerated as holy relics.

What were the lasting effects of the martyrs? Did they foster large-scale conversions of others? Did they strengthen the Christian cause over the long run? I see no evidence for such, though I fully concede that persecution, and the martyrdom that sometimes resulted from it, resulted in the loss of faithful people and in the destruction of early copies of the scriptures. If the ultimate measure of a person's faithfulness to God is found only in the cruel blood, fire, or wild beasts of martyrdom, those who for whatever reason are unwilling or unable to meet that terrible standard must consider themselves unworthy, irretrievably faulty and wanting. That does little to strengthen one's commitment to the Christian cause. Faced with the choice of death or sacrificing to the Roman gods, we know that many recanted their faith. Because so many Christians lapsed, the church soon was faced with the terrible dilemma of what to do with them. Were they to be forgiven or not? Did they require rebaptism before they could come back to the fold? Was the church a society of faithful saints or a school for weak sinners? The issues divided Christians for many years.

But did the Christians really have no alternatives? Was the choice that stark and simple: Recant or die? I doubt it, in most instances at least. Though the temptation to recant must have been strong indeed, perhaps Paul's words to the Saints at Corinth have application: "There hath no temptation taken you but such as is common to man: but God is faithful, who will not suffer you to be tempted above that ye are able; but will with the temptation also make a way to escape, that ye may be able to bear it. Wherefore, my dearly beloved, flee from idolatry" (1 Corinthians 10:13–14). I know that it's easy to espouse such a view from the safety and comfort of my quiet study, but even so, I'd like to hope that faced with the likelihood of martyrdom, there were more options open to Christians than to recant or die.

There is no doubt the lives of the martyrs have long since passed into the realms of mythology, such that it is very difficult to separate fact from fiction in any discussion of them. Many of the deeds attributed to them, to modern minds at least, strain credibility. Modern scholars believe that most of the gory stories about the martyrs are fictitious. Though millions of Christians over the centuries have prayed to blessed Saint So-and-so, and have believed fervently in the ability of martyrs to intercede with God, such beliefs, Latter-day Saints proclaim, are misguided at best. We respect those who believe that way; we just don't share their beliefs. Latter-day Saints proclaim that there is only one Advocate with the Father: Jesus Christ, the Redeeming Savior. "I am . . . your advocate with the Father," He has said (D&C 29:5; see also Mosiah 14:12; 15:8; Moroni 7:28). And if readers are unwilling to accept only Restoration scriptures to make the point, I refer them to a good Biblical source: "My little children, these things write I unto you, that ye sin not. And if any man sin, we have an advocate [Greek: intercessor, helper, comforter] with the Father, Jesus Christ the righteous: And he is the propitiation for our sins: and not for ours only, but also for the sins of the whole world" (1 John 2:1–2). And from John's gospel we read: "The Father . . . hath committed all judgment unto the Son" (John 5:22). Thus, Latter-day Saints pray to the Father, and *Him* only, and we pray in the name of the Son, and in *His* name only. Recall that Jesus taught us how to pray when He said: "After this manner therefore pray ye: Our Father which art in heaven" (Matthew 6:9). No intermediaries besides Christ, no matter their zeal or virtuous their lives, are required or desired.

I am of the view that the martyrs do not represent "the seed of the church," to quote half of Tertullian's famous phrase, no matter their personal popularity, their obvious courage, the admiration in which they have been held by most Christians, or the power of their rhetoric. The real seed of the church lies not in the blood of martyrs, but in the lives of countless faithful, believing, and behaving members. To be prepared to die for your faith, if needs be (as did Joseph Smith), is one thing. To actively seek death, to lust after it, is quite another. In fact, to lust after death, particularly in a way designed for maximum public attraction, is to my view a prideful and sinful act in and of itself. I just don't believe martyrs could legitimately claim God wanted them to engineer their own deaths, though many obviously thought that was so. I do believe that God, knowing they would be killed, gave them strength to get through their ordeal. Their physical courage was magnificent. However, God, the giver of life, is the One who measures the bounds of our mortality. Regardless of our motives, we have no right to destroy, in cold blood, and in the conscious exercise of self-will, that which we had no part in creating. In the words of President George Q. Cannon, "No one can destroy so precious a gift as that of life without incurring a severe penalty."[19]

While I stand in awe of their great courage, faith, and sincerity of purpose, to me the cult of the martyrs represents a church gone astray, retaining a form of godliness, but sadly not in tune with the Divine.

THE GREAT PERSECUTION

Until the middle of the third century, official Roman attitudes as set forth by the emperor remained that of Trajan in his answer to Pliny: "The Christians are not to be sought out." During most of that time, although there were localized outbreaks of persecution against Christians, they were not empire-wide or state-sponsored, and were often desultory in execution. Modern historians agree there were "long periods of tolerance and even friendship" between Christians and pagans.[20] The Roman authorities, I repeat, were less interested in making martyrs than in preserving and protecting the honor of the old gods of Rome. In the late A.D. 240s, Origen,[21] the celebrated Christian Biblical scholar and theologian, admitted that "'few' Christians had died for the faith, and then only when God thought the moment ripe." Because of their scarcity, "they were 'easily numbered,'" he said.[22]

But the third century brought unprecedented crisis to the Roman empire. The era of the "five good emperors" gave way to a prolonged period of civil war. This was the time of the "barracks emperors," a time when more than twenty different men ascended the imperial throne in the years between A.D. 235 and 284. Weakened by civil wars at home, the empire was unable to withstand the barbarians at the gates. Goths, Alamanni (a Germanic people), Franks, Saxons, and Sasanids, who, "like a swarm of bees," burst into Europe from the East. The Rhine and Danube barriers to the Roman empire were breached. The stresses and strains, which nearly destroyed the empire, raised old fears that the gods were withdrawing their favor from the Romans. Rome, it was feared, was being punished for its unfaithfulness. Nothing else could account for barbarians at the gates and civil war at home.

More out of desperation than anything else, the Roman authorities decided once more to appease the gods by offering them proper sacrifices. The emperor Decius, who reigned for only two years (he was killed by the Goths in A.D. 251), required that all citizens furnish proof of having offered sacrifice to the emperor. Enforcement was to be empire-wide, carried out by commissioners chosen by local city councils.

Jews were exempted from the imperial edict, but Christians, though not named explicitly, clearly were major targets and became its eventual victims. The edict was posted in mid-December of A.D. 249, and its effects were soon evident from Alexandria to Carthage. Many Christian leaders went into hiding. Others were taken, questioned, and executed or put in prison, eventually to be released. The authorities introduced a certificate which, if signed, attested that the signatory was one who sacrificed to the gods in the prescribed way. A copy of such a certificate, discovered in Egypt in 1893, is shown below. It is typical of the certificates signed by thousands of Christians.

To the commissioners for sacrifices in the village of Alexander's Island, from Aurelius Diogenes, son of Satabus, of the village of Alexander's Island, aged 72; scar on right eyebrow.

I have always sacrificed to the gods, and now in your presence, in accordance with the terms of the edict, I have done sacrifice and poured libations and tasted the sacrifices, and I request you to certify to this effect. Farewell.

Presented by me, Aurelius Diogenes

I certify that I witnessed his sacrifice, Aurelius Syrus

Dated this first year of the Emperor Caesar Gaius Messius Quintus Trajanus Decius, Pius, Felix, Augustus, the 2nd of Epiph. (26 June 250).[23]

Enforcement of the edict was haphazard at best, and corruption in its administration was widespread on all sides. In any event, after March A.D. 251, persecution seems to have dwindled away. The further the Decian persecution has receded into the past the more flamboyant are the legendary tales—almost all of them almost certainly fictitious—about its purported martyred victims.

But more significant problems for Christians were just over the horizon. As the third century came to a close, a new emperor, Diocletian, finally was able to stabilize the empire. An able soldier, but also a capable administrator, Diocletian created an absolute monarchy, with himself as the semi-divine ruler.

Recognizing that the empire was too large and cumbersome to be ruled by one man, and understanding that provincial governors were all too prone to participate in or at least acquiesce to rebellions, Diocletian divided the empire into Western and Eastern halves. He assumed direct control over the Eastern half and gave that of the West to an old colleague, Maximian. Each was assisted by a subordinate, known as a Caesar. This system, known as the Tetrarchy, soon failed, but Diocletian's division of the empire into two parts became permanent. Through all of the maneuvering, Diocletian was clearly the ultimate source of authority. He and his associates faced tremendous economic, social, and religious problems. To try to restore what he saw as the ancient discipline and virtue of Rome, and in hopes the gods would restore their blessings to the empire as in earlier times, Diocletian issued a decree in A.D. 303, which enjoined the demolition of Christian churches and the burning of Christian scriptures. Christian services were banned. Eusebius, the "Father of Church History," recorded the event as follows:

"It was enacted by their majesties Diocletian and Maximian that the meetings of Christians should be abolished. . . .

"March 303. . . . Imperial edicts were published everywhere ordering that the churches be razed to the ground, that the Scriptures be destroyed by fire, that those holding office be deposed and they of the household be deprived of freedom, if they persisted in the profession of Christianity. This was the first edict against us. But not long after other decrees were issued, which enjoined that the rulers of the churches in every place be first imprisoned, and thereafter every means be used to compel them to sacrifice.

"April 304. . . . Imperial edicts were issued, in which, by a general decree, it was ordered that all the people without exception should sacrifice in the several cities and offer libations to the idols."[24]

In some places, the edict commanding all people to sacrifice to the gods was enforced street by street, by armed soldiery. That happened in parts of the Eastern empire, but in the West this decree seems not to have been applied, though Western Christians were thrown out of their meeting places and had to surrender their scriptures.

Christians, particularly those in the Eastern part of the empire, continued to suffer for several years. In some cities, checks on Christians were carried out at the city gates and public baths; leaders and others were imprisoned, and some were killed. Many Christians lapsed, recanting their faith, and the church struggled to deal with them fairly.

But even in the Eastern empire the administration of the anti-Christian orders was uneven. Bribery of the authorities was common and conniving to get around the law was widespread. Modern historians agree that the "great persecution," while locally ferocious at times, was nowhere near as severe in its overall effects as Christian tradition asserts.

By the end of the third century, most people realized that the most lurid stories about supposed Christian vice and crime were false. Christianity had been around for a long time, and most people, who saw their Christian neighbors as harmless though probably a bit "odd," were not inclined to go after them with any real vigor. Furthermore, Christians had taken leading roles in treating the sick in the great epidemics that periodically swept the empire. In contrast, the pagans mostly did not. Survivors remembered and appreciated the Christians for their goodness.[25] Thus, the persecutions sputtered and flared up, only to die down again. It became clear that the empire would not be saved by killing all the Christians. Besides, there were by then too many of them to do so easily.

The Eastern Caesar, Galerius, had, so it is said, a deep hatred for Christians and did much to persuade his superior, Diocletian, to issue the edicts that inaugurated the eight years of "the great persecution." Galerius succeeded Diocletian as emperor when Diocletian abdicated in A.D. 305. On his deathbed, under political pressure from rivals, Galerius signed in A.D. 311 an Edict of Toleration. Lactantius, a convert to Christianity who later became tutor to the son of the Emperor Constantine, recorded that decree, which begrudgingly allows Christians the right to exist, provided "they do not offend against public order":

"Among our other regulations to promote the lasting good of the community we have hitherto endeavoured to restore a universal conformity to the ancient institutions and public order of the Romans; and in particular it has been our aim to bring back to a right disposition the Christians who had abandoned the religion of their fathers. . . . After the publication of our edict ordering the Christians to conform to the ancient institutions, many of them were brought to order through fear, while many were exposed to danger. Nevertheless, since many still persist in their opinions, and since we have observed that they now neither show due reverence to the gods nor worship their own God, we therefore, with our wonted clemency in extending pardon to all, are pleased to grant indulgence to these men, allowing Christians the right to exist again and to set up their places of worship; provided always that they do not offend against public order. We will in a further instruction explain to the magistrates how they should conduct themselves in this matter. In return for this indulgence of ours it will be the duty of Christians to pray to God for our recovery, for the public weal and for their own; that the state may be preserved from danger on every side, and that they themselves may dwell safely in their homes."[26]

Two years later, the Edict of Milan, signed by Constantine and Licinius, then but not for evermore co-emperors

(Constantine in the East and Licinius in the West), "agreed on a policy of religious freedom for all, Christians and pagans alike."[27] Lactantius recorded that agreement as follows:

"When we, Constantine and Licinius, Emperors, met at Milan in conference concerning the welfare and security of the realm, we decided that of the things that are of profit to all mankind, the worship of God ought rightly to be our first and chiefest care, and that it was right that Christians and all others should have freedom to follow the kind of religion they favoured; so that the God who dwells in heaven might be propitious to us and to all under our rule. We therefore announce that, notwithstanding any provisions concerning the Christians in our former instructions, all who choose that religion are to be permitted to continue therein, without any let or hindrance, and are not to be in any way troubled or molested. Note that at the same time all others are to be allowed the free and unrestricted practice of their religions; for it accords with the good order of the realm and the peacefulness of our times that each should have freedom to worship God after his own choice; and we do not intend to detract from the honour due to any religion or its followers. Moreover, concerning the Christians, we before gave orders with respect to the places set apart for their worship. It is now our pleasure that all who have bought such places should restore them to the Christians, without any demand for payment. . . .

"You are to use your utmost diligence in carrying out these orders on behalf of the Christians, that our command may be promptly obeyed, for the fulfilment of our gracious purpose in establishing public tranquillity. So shall that divine favour which we have already enjoyed, in affairs of the greatest moment, continue to grant us success, and thus secure the happiness of the realm."[28]

In time, the Christian triumph would extend even further.

But though it had won legal recognition, the church bore little resemblance to that in the apostolic period. Riven by desertion, torn apart by schismatic movements, espousing false beliefs and superstitions, lacking apostolic direction and supervision, it was in truth, I contend, an apostate organization.

NOTES

1. Pliny the Elder (A.D. 23–79), the uncle of Pliny the Younger (Governor of Bithynia-Pontus), was a celebrated Roman naturalist. His *Historia Naturalis,* written in A.D. 77, summarized a "general description of everything that is known to exist throughout the earth." It is a vast collection of nonsense and useful information. As noted in the text he died during an eruption of Mount Vesuvius.

2. *Documents of the Christian Church,* 3–4.

3. Fox, *Pagans and Christians,* 427.

4. Clement of Alexandria (circa A.D. 150–215) was a celebrated second- and third-century theologian and philosopher, thoroughly imbued with Greek philosophy, which he regarded as a divine gift to mankind.

5. Justin Martyr (circa A.D. 100–165) was an early Christian apologist, who sought to reconcile the claims of faith and reason. His writings are of great value in assessing the state of Christian liturgy in his time. He was martyred in Rome circa A.D. 165, and is now a saint of the Roman Catholic Church.

6. *Documents of the Christian Church,* 4.

7. Frend, *The Rise of Christianity,* 150.

8. Tacitus (circa A.D. 55–120) was a famous Roman historian, about whom surprisingly little is known. Only a few of his works have survived. His works provide the model used by Gibbon in his monumental *The History of the Decline and Fall of the Roman Empire.*

9. *Documents of the Christian Church,* 2.

10. See Fox, *Pagans and Christians,* 432.

11. See Cullmann, *Peter: Disciple, Apostle, Martyr,* 91–100; Brown and Meier, *Antioch and Rome,* 122–27. Garry Willis also notes that Clement of Rome, an early church leader writing near the end of the first century (circa A.D. 96), claims that the apostles were killed out of a "rivalrous grudge" (Wills, *Papal Sin,* 280). Wills also references Tacitus, the famed Roman historian, and observes that "Nero first took some Christians prisoner, who

explained that they were not responsible for the fire *but informed on others who were*" (ibid., emphasis in original).

12. Tertullian (circa A.D. 160–220) was a prominent African church leader and the author of a long list of theological works in Latin. He was a stout defender of "orthodoxy" against heretics, whom he declared had no right to interpret scripture. Many place him second only to Augustine in the top rank of Western theologians of the first five centuries A.D.

13. Quoted in Johnson, *A History of Christianity*, 71.

14. Frend, *The Rise of Christianity*, 148.

15. See Fox, *Pagans and Christians*, 433.

16. Ibid., 437.

17. *Documents of the Christian Church*, 9.

18. See Johnson, *A History of Christianity*, 72.

19. Cannon, *Gospel Truth*, 25.

20. McKay et al., *A History of World Societies*, 175.

21. See chapter 4, note 20, of this book.

22. Fox, *Pagans and Christians*, 434.

23. *Documents of the Christian Church*, 13.

24. Ibid., 14.

25. See Stark, *The Rise of Christianity*, 76–94.

26. *Documents of the Christian Church*, 15.

27. Chadwick, *The Early Church*, 122.

28. *Documents of the Christian Church*, 15–16.

CHAPTER SIX

CONSTANTINE AND THE GREAT COUNCIL

O N 28 OCTOBER A.D. 312, Constantine, one of the four "tetrarchs" who then ruled the Roman Empire, fought a battle that was, in retrospect, one of the turning points of history. Constantine was at the time a pagan who had grown up in the court of Diocletian, the major author of the "great persecution." Bold, vigorous, a master politician, both supremely confident and competent, he had broken with the fragile ruling coalition and launched himself and his legions across the Alps into an invasion of Italy. Now, at age 28, after an already brilliant military career, Constantine stood at the threshold of momentous historical change.

His opponent, Maxentius, had many more troops but foolishly left the shelter of the walls of Rome and ventured out to give battle in the open field. It was a day, stated Eusebius, when God intervened miraculously in human affairs.[1] Constantine proclaimed that the day before the battle he and "all the troops" had seen a sign of the cross in the noonday sky, inscribed with the words in Latin "by this conquer." That night, said Constantine's biographer, Eusebius, Constantine was visited in his dreams by

the figure of Jesus Christ, who bore the same symbol and commanded the emperor to use its likeness in the forthcoming battle
with his foes. Constantine had his troops paint the symbol of the
cross on their shields. The God of the Christians, he was sure,
favored him.

The ensuing battle, known as the battle of the Milvian
Bridge, soon was decided in Constantine's favor. Maxentius, flee-
ing the scene, drowned in the Tiber, and Constantine established
himself with Licinius (his brother-in-law) as joint emperor. The
Edict of Milan, issued by the two of them the next year, A.D. 313,
gave unrestricted freedom to the Christians and provided for
complete restoration of all church property still remaining in the
hands of the state or of individuals after the persecutions of the
previous decade. Though it did not "establish" the church, the
edict signaled the end of persecution. Whether out of gratitude,
fear, or in hopes of future benefits, Constantine was beginning to
pay back the debt he felt he owed to the God of the Christians.

By September A.D. 324, Constantine had defeated his
remaining rival, Licinius, who soon turned up dead, profession-
ally strangled, probably at Constantine's order. Constantine was
henceforth the sole ruler of the Roman world. From then on,
there would be no "live and let live" relationship between the
Christian God and the old gods of Rome. The empire would,
over time, become Christian *and* Roman. Or so, at least,
Constantine concluded. Constantine became the imperial patron
of the Christians, but he chose to recognize only that group of
them that was the largest and best organized, a group he called
"the lawful and most holy Catholic [international] Church."[2] In
time, he would suppress all others.

Soon vast benefits began to accrue to the church and its
officials. Church officers became privileged, not persecuted.
Members of the clergy became authorized to serve as civic officers, with the same jurisdiction as magistrates, able to hear cases

as though they were a secular tribunal, including the right to release slaves from their servitude. Meeting places belonging to Christians were restored to them "without payment and without any demand for compensation," and without any delay. Generous grants of money were provided to Christian ministries, and an Eastern bishop was advised not to "hesitate to ask . . . for whatever [funds] you find necessary." But all of these benefits were available only to ministers of the "lawful and most holy Catholic Church." All others got short shrift. Under Constantine's patronage, the boundaries of the orthodox faith were being established—in fits and starts, to be sure—and state-church relationships that would determine Western history for a thousand years were beginning to jell.

Historians have debated endlessly over whether Constantine truly was converted to Christianity, or whether he simply used it for his own political purposes.[3] Without question, Constantine believed he had found in Christ an all-powerful patron, whose favor he would be wise to seek after and maintain. Yet he continued, at least initially, to support paganism, even though he *may* have had a personal conviction that the Christian God favored him. His personal beliefs remain controversial, elusive. Was he the first Christian emperor or just a shrewd opportunist? Perhaps he exhibited elements of both. He cared little about the theological differences between various Christian groups; though he "favoured Christianity among the many religions of his subjects, . . . [he] did not make it the official or 'established' religion of the empire."[4] What he wanted was peace and quiet in the empire, with his own position fully secure. If the Christians could help him attain and maintain necessary unity and domestic peace, so much the better. Constantine was quite prepared to suppress dissent, with ferocious intensity if need be, in the interest of imperial unity, and, not least, in the maintenance of his own imperial position and power. With Constantine, other considerations came second. He treated Christian bishops as though he owned them: summoning them, enforcing whatever opinions the majority of them decided upon, less interested in what was decided than that unity prevailed. Christian doctrine was never allowed to take precedence over affairs of state or political advantage.

There is no doubt Constantine was impressed by many aspects of Christian morality. Their peacefulness, their humble acceptance of the trials and troubles of mortality in the hope of happiness beyond the grave, their emphasis on faithful marriage and family life, their submission to the secular power—these and other admirable qualities could, Constantine knew, be of great value to him in purifying, strengthening, and reinvigorating the empire, even restoring its ancient virtues and discipline.

Throughout his reign Constantine, a consummate politician, continued to play to both pagan and Christian sensibilities. In his exhortations he used vague monotheistic language that both pagans and Christians could embrace. He was careful not to antagonize the army, which remained largely non-Christian. He restored pagan temples as he built Christian churches. He continued to pay public homage to the sun, *sol invictus*. In dedicating his new capital, Constantinople, he used both pagan and Christian rites.

But over time, as his power base became more secure, Constantine came out more and more in favor of the Christian cause. He gradually shifted the allegiance of the empire from the old "immortal gods" of Rome to the Christian God. The cynic would say that the Christians won the day because of imperial patronage. But in truth the Christian message had broad mass appeal. Many who had hung back in harder times, fearful of persecution, now pressed for baptism and sought public allegiance with Christianity. It was now safe to do so.

Money was given to needy Christian congregations, and Christian bishops were authorized to distribute food to the poor from the imperial grain supply. Churches were given vast endowments of land and wealth, and church lands were exempted from taxation. Bequests to the church were legalized and encouraged. It became both politically correct and profitable to be Christian.

At the same time, however, meetings of heretical Christians were banned, and the rights of the Jews were restricted, as Christian prejudices against the Jews became translated into legal liabilities for the latter.

Constantine's personal life was hardly in keeping with Christian morality. Though he got along well with his mother, Helena, Constantine ordered the execution of his son, Crispus, his nephew Licinianus, and his second wife, Fausta.[5] After their deaths, his mother, Helena, emerged as the doyenne of the imperial court. She championed Christianity and traveled to Palestine distributing gifts, claiming to have found the "true cross." At the end of his life, after reigning thirty years, Constantine was baptized, a sacrament he purposely had deferred until that time, in recognition of the compromises required of rulers and in hopes he could leave this world washed clean from his sins. Historian Will Durant indicates there are "signs that remorse weighed heavily on his declining years." Still, give him full credit for associating an aging empire with a vigorous young religion. As Durant notes: "By [Constantine's] aid Christianity became a state as well as a church, and the mold, for fourteen centuries, of European life and thought."[6]

THE FACADE OF CHRISTIAN UNITY IS SHATTERED: THE DONATIST SCHISM

Constantine soon became deeply involved in matters of discipline within the church, matters that had there been apostolic direction would have been dealt with locally by internal administrative procedures, not by an autocratic and heavy-handed emperor who was not even a church member. Pent-up tensions within the Christian church in North Africa burst into the open, focusing on how to deal with clergy who had recanted their Christian allegiance under earlier Roman persecution. A volatile and zealous priest named Donatus, who had himself survived torture and imprisonment by the Romans, but had not been broken by them, opposed the return of priests and bishops he considered traitors, men who had succumbed to Roman coercion, perhaps even betrayed others. He felt they had lost their ability to perform their priestly functions in a valid manner, and were, in truth, a stench in the nostrils of God. Corrupt clergymen, the Donatists believed, could not function as God's representatives. In their view of things, even lay persons who had lapsed during the persecution would have to show extraordinary repentance before they could return to the Christian fold.

Since large numbers of Christians, clergy and lay persons alike, had folded under Roman pressure, many bishops felt this rigorous and puritanical position was more than a little extreme. Most just wanted to put the bad times behind them, to forgive and forget. After all, most clergy had themselves made compromises of one sort or another, to save their own skins. Behind that view was the dubious principle that a priest's personal holiness had little to do with his right to perform priestly functions. The Donatists just couldn't embrace that idea.

The bad feelings between the "betrayers" (the *traditores*) and those who had remained faithful, compounded by interprovincial rivalries and personal bickerings, soon threatened to tear the North African church apart. Caecilian, bishop at Carthage, was accused by other bishops of having been consecrated by a bishop who had himself been a *traditore*, and a council of other bishops deposed Caecilian and elected another in his place. The replacement bishop supposedly was free from the taint of having been a traitor to the Christian cause. The Donatists set up rival bishops whenever the existing prelates did not meet their exacting standards.

Dismayed by the thought that Christianity might not be the unifying force he had hoped for, Constantine got into the middle of the fight. He appointed a panel of bishops from Gaul and Italy to investigate the matter and report back to him. Their report, which favored the opponents of the Donatists, was appealed on the basis that many of the "judges" had themselves been traitors in previous years. So Constantine asked another tribunal, consisting of 33 bishops and 13 other clergy, with judges personally selected by him, to meet in A.D. 314 at Arles, in Gaul. This was the first general council ever held in the Western church, and the first that gathered under the patronage of the emperor. Their report, which again went against the Donatists, brought no peace. Constantine was angry. Why, oh, why couldn't these Christians just get along together? Didn't they understand that lack of unity might offend God *and* weaken Constantine's favor with the Almighty? He took matters into his own hands, declaring that as supreme magistrate and *pontifex maximus* (chief priest) of the empire, he would make the decision himself. He, and he alone, would serve as God's representative. He would have unity even if he had to force it on those too obstinate to reach it of their own accord. He ruled against the Donatists, confiscating their property and exiling their leaders.

But most of the North African bishops were neither impressed nor cowed. They viewed Constantine as one who used money and gifts to undermine the faithful. The state, they felt, remained in hostile relationship to the church, despite all the flattery and bribery used by Constantine. His resort to force had failed, not just because the North Africans disliked being pushed around by him, but also because the North African church felt that profound social and religious grievances existed between it and other parts of the Christian West. Five years later,

Constantine threw in the towel. Never again would he try to beat into submission a dissident faction. The Donatists continued to prosper in Africa, but the unity of the Western church was shattered. The power of the civil authority had been used to enforce orthodoxy, and that not for the last time.

A century after the controversy, the Donatist and mainstream churches of North Africa remained locked in civil war. Augustine, the celebrated bishop of Hippo in the fifth century, advocated violent suppression of the Donatists, including mass killings if needed. Only when invading Vandals suppressed all North African churches, Donatists and orthodox alike, did the conflict end.

Constantine soon faced the most challenging threat to orthodoxy in the first thousand years of church history, a controversy that swirled through society for centuries, dividing churches and communities, fostering lynch mobs, and raising tempers to the boiling point in a dozen parts of the empire. Around A.D. 318, Alexander, the bishop of Alexandria, heard that Arius, a popular cleric in a wealthy parish in that city, had been preaching that the Christ, the Word of God, was not only subordinate to the Father, but having been "begotten" must necessarily have had a beginning of existence, and a time, therefore, when He was not. If the Word was made *ex nihilo* (from nothing), He must then be a "creature," and not as is the Father "alone unbegotten, alone eternal and alone without beginning," as Arius said.[7] Such a "creature," Alexander feared, could not have been fully God, and certainly would not be capable of redeeming mankind.

Heresy of this magnitude could not be permitted. Alexander convoked a council of bishops, which condemned Arius and exiled him. But Arius had important and influential friends, and strong pro-Arian camps soon arose, particularly in the Eastern churches in the Roman provinces of Bithynia, Asia, and Cyrenaica. Many bishops there had no quarrel with Arian ideas.

Constantine soon heard of the troubles in Egypt. His concerns were not theological but related to the need for unity. Christianity was to be the single religion of the empire, and that being so, Constantine wanted squabbling and bickering to stop. Frivolous debates between rival philosophers (which is what Constantine considered Arius and Alexander to be) and hashing and rehashing trivial (to Constantine) theological differences had no place in the emperor's agenda: he wanted sweet dreams at night, and glorious peace each day.

Constantine, ever ready to settle disputes, by force if needs be, decided to act as mediator. A universal church council would do the trick, he felt. Every problem afflicting the church, including the question of Arius, the dating of Easter, and the best way to deal with schismatic groups could then be settled. And once settled, unity, blessed unity, would at last prevail, and Constantine's troubles would be over. Or so he thought.

THE GREAT COUNCIL

And so the Great Council was called, to be held at a pleasant town on a lake, a place called Nicaea in Bithynia, a part of the empire where Arian ideas were not only popular but held by many to be fully orthodox.[8] The fact that Constantine's summer palace was there, with plenty of room for everyone, made the choice of location even more attractive. About 250 bishops, most from the Eastern part of the empire, with associated clergy and other retainers, arrived, and Constantine himself opened the proceedings on 20 May, A.D. 325. The *lingua franca* spoken by all was Greek.

No written records of the debates held during the Council have survived. There seems, however, to have been more heat than light generated. Few were prepared to listen to Arius's tightly reasoned, philosophy-tinged arguments. Most would have been prepared to accept "almost any formula which would secure harmony within the church," as Timothy Barnes has pointed out.[9]

A traditional story about the Council, which of course cannot be confirmed because there are no written records of the proceedings, but which one would hope to be true, indicates that bishops skilled in the Greek arts of rhetoric, debate, and philosophy dominated the first session. Finally, one of the Egyptian clerics, an old man who had sat patiently listening to empty eloquence, rose to speak. He had been blinded and crippled by Diocletian's torturers. "Know you not," he said, "that Christ and his Apostles left us not a system of logic, nor a vain deceit, but a naked truth, to be guarded by faith and good works."[10] One can only imagine the silence that must have fallen over the assembly as those in attendance felt the tug of truth lead them—if only momentarily—away from philosophy and the fallacies inherent in human reasoning to the simple majesty of faith.

Alexander and his protégé, Athanasius, the bishop's young, intense secretary, who soon became the standard-bearer for the "orthodox" view, hammered away at the need to define Christianity in a way that would clearly brand Arius's views as heretical and thus unacceptable, without driving away the Eastern bishops, many of whom were sympathetic to the Arian position. Constantine himself, we are told, introduced a term, *homoousious,* which defined the Son as "consubstantial" (one being) with the Father. That would make the Son essentially no different than the Father, so it was thought. Since the phrase does not appear in the scriptures and had not been used in Christian tradition either, some bishops thought it extreme and unwise to require its acceptance by the entire church. Still, to define the Trinity as "three persons in one substance," though it introduced as many theological problems as it solved, might at least provide the formula for some sort of agreement and allow everyone to go home.

And the words were ambiguous enough in meaning to be interpreted differently by Arians and anti-Arians.

More importantly, perhaps, Constantine had weighed in on the matter, and who dared to gainsay him? Who would be so bold as to declare the emperor a heretic? Constantine, frustrated by theological wrangling, anxious above all else for unity, urged acceptance of Christ's nature as of "one being with" the Father. Let's just end the argument, was his view. And so they did, for a while at least. Arius and his views were declared anathema. All who were present signed the document, except for a couple of bishops who remained loyal to Arius and left with him, one would suppose, in a huff.

The text of the Nicene Creed, which from henceforth defined orthodox Christianity, became sacrosanct, immutable. It reads as follows: "We believe in one God the Father All-sovereign, maker of all things visible and invisible; and in one Lord Jesus Christ, the Son of God, begotten of the Father, only-begotten, that is the substance of the Father, God of God, Light of Light, true God of true God, by whom all things were made, things in heaven and things on the earth; who for us men and for our salvation came down and was made flesh, and became man, suffered, and rose on the third day, ascended into heaven, and is coming to judge living and dead. And in the Holy Spirit. And those that say, 'There was when he was not,' and 'Before he was begotten he was not,' and that, 'He came into being from what-is-not,' or those that allege, that the Son of God is 'of another substance or essence' or 'created' or 'changeable' or 'alterable,' these the Catholic and Apostolic Church anathematizes."[11]

Having neatly disposed of the concerns about the nature of God—or so he must have thought—Constantine had the bishops set a date for Easter, which separated it from the Jewish Passover.

After two months of work and a sumptuous closing banquet,

Constantine sent the bishops home, secure in his belief that "we have received from divine Providence the blessing of being freed from all error, and united in the acknowledgement of one and the same faith. The devil will no longer have any power over us. . . . Wherefore we all worship the one true God and believe that he is."[12]

But of course it was not to be. And how, in retrospect, could anyone think otherwise? The traditional "orthodox" view of God as wholly "other," immaterial, immutable, without body, parts or passions, is extra-scriptural. The creed raises as many questions as it solves.

Was it all, at the end, just the playing of power politics, the triumph of compromise over principle? Was it all about power— the power of the emperor in this world echoing that of God in heaven? Is it significant, as one historian has suggested, that "Arius's formulation, which acknowledges the Father's priority over the Son, survived for centuries in altered form in some of the Eastern churches, which tended to accept imperial power over church affairs, and later would influence the structure of what became 'state churches'"?[13]

Whatever else, as the next chapter shows, intense armed conflict and mob violence were common between Arians and anti-Arians in the decades after the Nicene Council supposedly had settled the issue of God's identity and Christ's relationship to the Father, once and for all time. These quarrels divided bishops and congregations for decades—some would say centuries—to come. Even Athanasius, who may have thought he had obtained a clear victory at Nicea, was deposed by a council of bishops within a few years, and the decision to throw him out was ratified by Constantine himself. After Constantine died in A.D. 337, Athanasius reclaimed his position, but later was again deposed twice. His third successful rival, the Arian bishop George of Cappadocia, who presided at Alexandria, was beaten to death by an enraged mob of Athanasians, and Athanasius managed, one last time, to hang on to his bishopric until he too died in A.D. 373. We will learn much more about Athanasius in the next chapter.

Of one thing we can however be certain: after the Council of Nicea, the bishops assumed hitherto-unknown power in the political as well as religious spheres. Church councils, held under the guidance and direction of the emperor, and bowing to his will, became the defining assemblies of orthodoxy. And it was not long before the church, which had suffered so much persecution, began itself to persecute others considered by it to be outside the realm of orthodoxy. The church's work of persecution was made possible by its close ties to the secular power, which often provided the "muscle" needed for enforcement.

In the years and centuries following the Council of Nicea, more than twenty ecumenical councils were held at various times and places. They considered a broad variety of subjects. At the Council of Chalcedon in A.D. 451, for example, those present drew up a statement of faith, the so-called *Chalcedonian Definition,* which reaffirmed the Definitions of Nicea (A.D. 325), and Constantinople (A.D. 381), asserting them to be a sufficient account of the orthodox faith regarding the doctrine of Christ. The Council of Chalcedon also sowed the seeds of future discord between the Eastern and Western churches by bestowing on the bishop of Constantinople the title of Patriarch, with the clear indication that there would be complete equality between the sees of Rome and Constantinople. The Eastern provinces of the empire would be responsible to the Patriarch alone. The ecclesiastical rivalry sown at Chalcedon would bear bitter fruits in the coming centuries.

Twelve centuries later, in a much different world, the Council of Trent (A.D. 1545–63) attempted to provide the Catholic response to the Protestant reformation. The Niceno-Constantinopolitan Creed was formally reaffirmed as a basis of faith. The

doctrine of transubstantiation was affirmed, and Protestant doctrine concerning the Eucharist (the sacrament of the Lord's
Supper) was repudiated.

But any consideration of the councils and the creeds they
produced over the centuries must deal with a vitally important
central issue: the theology and practices that the councils arrived
at were drastically different from those of the New Testament
period, when the church was under apostolic direction. In large
part, the councils got it wrong not just because there was so
much politicking and bad faith evidenced at them, and not
because the participants didn't try to reach a common understanding, but because the creeds they produced exhibit profound
differences in both language and concepts from those in the
scriptures. Their adoption resulted in a body of theology that was
acceptable to the gentile Greek world, but departed in significant
ways from the simple gospel message of Jesus and His apostles.
How ironic it is to note that over time, rejection of the concilia-
tory creeds came to be considered by the "orthodox" church as a
greater deterrent to Christian fellowship than rejection of the
New Testament itself!

GREEK PHILOSOPHY AND
CHRISTIAN THEOLOGY

The influence of Greek philosophy on Christian theology,
including concerns about the nature of God, which so preoccu-
pied the participants in the Council of Nicea, can hardly be
overemphasized. The Greek influence on religious thought was
profoundly positive in some ways. Greek thinkers such as Plato
and Aristotle moved people away from the immoral and capricious gods of the pantheon to nobler and more adequate conceptions of divinity. Maurice Wiles has noted that "all Christian
thinking, and especially all Christian thinking about the being

and nature of God, was influenced, often unconsciously, by philosophical ideas current in the Hellenistic world."[14] And Edwin Hatch's observation of over a century ago still holds true: "A large part of what are sometimes called Christian doctrines, and many usages which have prevailed and continue to prevail in the Christian Church, are in reality Greek theories and Greek usages changed in form and colour by the influence of primitive Christianity, but in their essence Greek still."[15]

Justin Martyr, a practicing philosopher of the Platonic school before he became a Christian in the second century, was the first Christian thinker to seek to reconcile the claims of faith and reason. He believed portions of the truth were found in Greek philosophy, but that Christianity was the only completely rational creed. Plato's teacher, Socrates, Justin averred, was in effect a "Christian before Christ."[16]

Justin used his philosophical training to defend Christianity against the Gnostics, sadly without great success. Many of his writings were directed towards Roman intellectuals and political leaders (including the emperor), who believed strongly in the role of philosophy in living a virtuous life. Christian doctrine, Justin claimed, was "more lofty than all human philosophy." Justin was martyred in Rome, probably in A.D. 164, after having refused to sacrifice to the Roman gods.

Toward the end of the second century, Greek philosophy began to exert a significant impact on Christian thought and teaching. Clement of Alexandria (A.D. 150–215),[17] who led the way in integrating Christian faith with the best secular thinking of the day, saw Platonism as a divine gift from God to mankind, wholly compatible with Christian and Jewish teachings, and an ally of Christianity. Platonism, Clement believed, was given by God to the Greeks to prepare them to receive Christ, just as the law of Moses had been given to the Jews as a "schoolmaster," for the same purpose. Plato, he said, was an imitation of Moses.

Clement drew upon the earlier works of the Alexandrian Jew Philo (circa 20 B.C.–A.D. 50), the most important figure among the Hellenistic Jews of his age. Philo developed an allegorical interpretation of scripture, which led him to see much of Greek philosophy in the Old Testament. Like Philo, Clement argued for an allegorical reading of the scriptures, rejecting literalism, and finding in such a view of Holy Writ philosophical teachings that buttressed and strengthened the Christian position. Clement's student Origen carried on the process of bringing Greek philosophy into the mainstream of Christian theology.[18] In the absence of divine revelation, Christian thinkers increasingly turned to Greek philosophy to assist them in rebutting the claims of heretics, particularly the dangerous, sophisticated Gnostics. Philosophy, it was felt, helped to formalize and institutionalize Christian doctrine and practices. By the time of the Council of Nicea, much of the theological debate that led to the framing of "orthodox" doctrine was being carried out in Platonic language, using Platonic assumptions.

Tertullian, a North African convert to the church (circa A.D. 150–212), who spent most of his life in Carthage, was horrified by Clement's philosophical approach to Christian theology.[19] He believed Platonism was evil and that philosophy lay at the root of apostasy. Tertullian devoted much of his legal skill to defending orthodoxy and mercilessly attacking Clement. He found little truth useful to Christianity outside of the revelations given to ancient Israel and through Jesus Christ. Tertullian's views on the nature of Christ and on the Trinity laid the foundation for orthodox views on these matters in both Eastern and Western churches.

It is important, in considering this brief overview of the effects of Greek philosophy on Christian theology, to keep in mind the chronology involved. Greek philosophy did not cause the apostasy. By the time Greek thought became an important factor in Christian theology, the apostasy had already occurred. Many Latter-day Saints do not understand this fact. Greek philosophy *was* integrated into Christian theology, but it occurred *after* the apostasy had already taken place, primarily in response to the dangerous teachings of schismatic groups in the third century.

THE NATURE OF GOD

To some of the Greek philosophers the idea that God has a body of flesh and bones was utterly incomprehensible and logically unacceptable. It was, to them, repugnant nonsense. The Neo-Platonist thinker Plotinus[20] (circa 205–270 A.D.), for example, though perhaps extreme in his views, was reputed to be ashamed that his soul had a body and "could not endure to discuss his lineage, nor his parents, nor his fatherland"![21] Early Christians, on the other hand, like the Jews who were their contemporaries, commonly and perhaps generally believed in an embodied God. As Christian apologists attempted to reconcile Greek philosophy with Christian beliefs, it was not long before the corporeal nature of God came under attack. Clement of Alexandria was perhaps the first Christian writer to declare that God is immaterial. That doctrine was taken up and expanded by Origen. Divine corporeality, Origen declared, is logically incompatible with Platonic conceptions of the nature of God, and therefore it cannot be. Such thought gives credence to Nephi's inspired observation that "when [men] are learned they think they are wise, and they hearken not unto the counsel of God, for they set it aside, supposing they know of themselves, wherefore, their wisdom is foolishness and it profiteth them not" (2 Nephi 9:28).

Tertullian countered such apostate teachings, insisting that God is embodied and resisting attempts by the immaterialists to

Platonize this aspect of Christian doctrine. The body was considered by Tertullian to be sacred, not shameful.

By the early part of the fifth century A.D., most Christian theologians had embraced the apostate Neoplatonic view that God is immaterial. Augustine, for example, was an uncompromising advocate of the incorporeity of God. Gradually, as Platonism became firmly ensconced as the dominant Christian worldview, the idea that God has a body faded away. As Professor David L. Paulsen has said, "The confluence of Christian and Greek thought in the first five centuries of the church would devastate the theological landscape for many more centuries to come. Some truths would be altered, others, like Divine embodiment, would be completely flipped on their head. There had occurred a turning away from the truth, an apostasy, which dealt such a blow to the gospel that no reformation could piece together the once perfect mosaic. It would require a complete restoration of truth and doctrine. Such a restoration would take place in the early 19th century."[22]

Yes, indeed: The church had reached such a state that though it retained "a form of godliness," it was in fact "teaching for doctrines the commandments of men" (Joseph Smith–History 1:14). That in part is why a revelatory restoration would be needed to restore the truth and divine authority and approbation.

LATTER-DAY SAINT VIEWS ON THE NATURE OF GOD

Latter-day Saints reject both sides of the argument supposedly settled by the Council of Nicea. Neither Arius nor Athanasius was without error. As President Gordon B. Hinckley has said, "We do not accept the Nicene Creed, nor any other creed based on tradition and the conclusions of men."[23] Latter-day Saints believe, along with other Christians, in a Godhead of

Father, Son, and Holy Ghost. However, we deny the nonbiblical idea that the members of the Godhead are one metaphysical substance. Though perfectly united, they are distinct individuals. Thus, we testify, as Elder Dallin H. Oaks has indicated, that "these three members of the Godhead are three separate and distinct beings. We also testify that God the Father is not just a spirit but is a glorified person with a tangible body, as is his resurrected Son, Jesus Christ. . . . The Nicene Creed erased the idea of the separate being of Father and Son by defining God the Son as being of 'one substance with the Father.'"[24]

Elder James E. Talmage explained the Latter-day Saint concept of the unity of God, which though asserting that the Godhead consists of three separate Beings, speaks also to their perfect and complete unity of thought, purpose, and operation. He said:

"This unity is a type of completeness; the mind of any one member of the Trinity is the mind of the others; seeing as each of them does with the eye of perfection, they see and understand alike. Under any given conditions each would act in the same way, guided by the same principles of unerring justice and equity. The one-ness of the Godhead, to which the scriptures so abundantly testify, implies no mystical union of substance, nor any unnatural and therefore impossible blending of personality. Father, Son, and Holy Ghost are as distinct in their persons and individualities as are any three personages in mortality. Yet their unity of purpose and operation is such as to make their edicts one, and their will the will of God."[25]

Though it may seem to be nothing more than theological nit-picking, concern about the nature of God is of grave importance. The Prophet Joseph Smith understood that. He said, "It is the first principle of the gospel to know for a certainty the character of God, and to know that we may converse with Him as one man converses with another."[26] In that same sermon, the

King Follett Discourse, given on 7 April 1844 the Prophet also said, "If men do not comprehend the character of God, they do not comprehend themselves."[27]

Latter-day Saint views on the nature and character of God rest firmly and forever on the validity of the First Vision vouchsafed to the Prophet Joseph Smith. President Gordon B. Hinckley stated the position clearly and simply:

"We do accept, as the basis of our doctrine, the statement of the Prophet Joseph Smith that when he prayed for wisdom in the woods, 'the light rested upon me [and] I saw two Personages, whose brightness and glory defy all description, standing above me in the air. One of them spake unto me, calling me by name and said, pointing to the other—*This is my Beloved Son. Hear Him!'* (Joseph Smith—History 1:17).

"Two beings of substance were before him. He saw them. They were in form like men, only much more glorious in their appearance. He spoke to them. They spoke to him. They were not amorphous spirits. Each was a distinct personality. They were beings of flesh and bone whose nature was reaffirmed in later revelations which came to the Prophet.

"Our entire case as members of The Church of Jesus Christ of Latter-day Saints rests on the validity of this glorious First Vision. It was the parting of the curtain to open this, the dispensation of the fulness of times. Nothing on which we base our doctrine, nothing we teach, nothing we live by is of greater importance than this initial declaration. I submit that if Joseph Smith talked with God the Father and His Beloved Son, then all else of which he spoke is true. This is the hinge on which turns the gate that leads to the path of salvation and eternal life.

"Are we Christians? Of course we are Christians. We believe in Christ. We worship Christ. We take upon ourselves in solemn covenant His holy name. The Church to which we belong carries His name. He is our Lord, our Savior, our Redeemer through whom came the great Atonement with salvation and eternal life."[28]

NOTES

1. Eusebius, *The History of the Church from Christ to Constantine*, 291–96.
2. Ibid., 323–24, 326–27.
3. See Sordi, *The Christians and the Roman Empire*, 133–43.
4. Chadwick, *The Early Church*, 127.
5. See Durant, *Caesar and Christ*, 663.
6. Ibid., 664.
7. Quoted in Frend, *The Rise of Christianity*, 494.
8. See Rubenstein, *When Jesus Became God*, 68–88.
9. Barnes, *Constantine and Eusebius*, 215.
10. Romer, *Testament*, 217.
11. Quoted in Frend, *The Rise of Christianity*, 499.
12. Ibid., 500.
13. Pagels, *Beyond Belief*, 175.
14. Wiles, *The Making of Christian Doctrine*, 28.
15. Hatch, *The Influence of Greek Ideas and Usage upon the Christian Church*, 350.
16. See Olson, *The Story of Christian Theology*, 58–59; see also chapter 5, note 5, of this book.
17. See Olson, *Story of Christian Theology*, 86–90; see also chapter 5, note 4, of this book.
18. See Olson, *Story of Christian Theology*, 99–112; see also chapter 4, note 20, of this book.
19. See Olson, *Story of Christian Theology*, 90–98; see also chapter 5, note 12, of this book.
20. Plotinus (circa 205–270 A.D.), a noted Neoplatonic philosopher and mystic, who worked in Rome, had a profound influence on Augustine and hence on the theologians of the Middle Ages. He believed the Divine existed in three separate entities. Plotinus claimed to have produced a synthesis of Stoic ethics and Aristotelian logic within a Platonic framework.
21. Romer, *Testament*, 209.
22. Paulsen, "The God of Primitive Christianity: Apostasy and Restoration," 24; see also Paulsen, "Early Christian Belief in a Corporeal Deity: Origen and Augustine as Reluctant Witnessess," 105–16; Paulsen, "Must

God Be Incorporeal?" 76–87; Griffin and Paulsen, "Augustine and the Corporeality of God," 97–118.

  23. Hinckley, "What Are People Asking about Us?" 71.
  24. Oaks, "Apostasy and Restoration," 84, 85.
  25. Talmage, *A Study of the Articles of Faith,* 37.
  26. *History of the Church,* 6:305.
  27. Ibid., 6:303.
  28. Hinckley, "What Are People Asking about Us?" 71.

CHAPTER SEVEN

THE CORRUPTION OF POWER

W ITH ITS ALL-TOO-EAGER EMBRACE of wealth and power, the post-Nicene church hierarchy soon began to act like ecclesiastical counterparts of Roman potentates.

Within a few short years, bishops were dressing in elaborate, bejeweled finery, decked out in the rich robes of Roman courtiers. Ammianus, a pagan but fair-minded historian writing fifty years after the Nicene Council, noted that once in office the bishops of Rome were "free from money worries, enriched by offerings from married women, riding in carriages, dressing splendidly, feasting luxuriantly—their banquets are better than imperial ones."[1] Over time, the bishops of Rome assumed the title of pope ("papa," or "father"). In A.D. 1073, Pope Gregory VII, in a council at Rome, formally prohibited use of the term *pope* by any other bishop than the bishop of Rome.

Church buildings became models of the imperial court of the emperor: "Our walls glitter with gold," wrote Jerome[2] (A.D. 342–420), "and gold gleams upon our ceilings and the capitals of our pillars; yet Christ is dying at our doors in the person of his poor, naked and hungry."[3]

Bibles, written on purple-stained vellum in inks of gold and silver, were bound in gold and precious jewels, carried in solemn processions, and, like the hem on the emperor's cloak, kissed by the faithful. They were to be venerated, not read.

At the same time the gap between the clergy, by now a full-time paid occupation, and the common people widened, as did that between bishops and priests. Thus, Arian bishops, though they supported Arius doctrinally, distanced themselves from him personally because he was only a priest and *they* were bishops!

The church hierarchy, in short, acted like the mirror image of the imperial court. Even its term for the church's territorial unit of administration, the diocese, was borrowed from the Roman Empire.

All in all, this jostling for pomp and power represented a complete reversal from the humility of Jesus, the Good Shepherd; Peter, the simple fisherman; or Paul, the humble tentmaker, each of whom had been the servant of all.

In his revealing tale of the Nicene Council and the world thereafter, Richard E. Rubenstein notes that "Christian bishops, while expected to be pure and peaceful men, were now among the most powerful political figures in the empire. The contradictions between the ideals of behavior represented by Jesus Christ's life and the requirements for holding office in the fourth-century Church were agonizing. The bishops' worldly duties and ambitions often involved them in political intrigue, financial chicanery, abuse of legal processes, and sheer thuggery against their opponents—all of which might generate charges to be used against them by political or doctrinal enemies. Moreover, since they were now servants of the emperor, churchmen like Eustathius [the anti-Arian bishop of Antioch; lived A.D. 300–377] could be accused of *lèse majesté* (insulting the sovereign, in this case, Constantine's mother), or worse. Soon, bishops on both sides of the Arian controversy would be defending themselves against charges of outright treason."[4]

Eustathius, it must be noted, soon was convicted by his Arian enemies on charges of an illicit sexual relationship with a woman not his wife, excommunicated, deposed from office, and after being questioned by Constantine himself, sent into exile. Rubenstein points out that while there is no evidence fourth-century church leaders were particularly corrupt or venal men, their standards of ethical behavior were riddled with contradictions. The issue of priestly celibacy was yet unsettled, and many priests and bishops were married. The Council of Nicea had ordered all clergy to get women other than their mothers and sisters out of their houses, but little attention was paid to this edict. Consequently, any cleric involved with a woman, even if licitly, and even if she were his legal wife, ran the risk of someone claiming sexual misconduct. Still, it would be naive to think there was no substance to any of the stories, human behavior being what it is.

Violent and most definitely un-Christian behavior among competing factions within the church remained common for many years, as uninspired but ambitious men jostled for power. Athanasius, the supposed victor of Nicea, was the target of many charges relating to his actions and those of his supporters. On one occasion, bishops from one faction, the Melitians, complained bishop Athanasius had sent violent gangs to beat and harass their followers and refused to let them worship in their churches even though the Council of Nicea had agreed the Melitians had authority to act as Christian clergy.[5] Charges of corrupt administration, including extortion, soon followed. Then, most seriously, one of Athanasius's thugs beat up a clergyman he considered to have questionable credentials, overturned the altar of his church, and committed sacrilege by breaking a sacred chalice used to celebrate the Eucharist. Even worse, Athanasius was accused of giving gold to a court official suspected of plotting against Constantine. Strangely, perhaps, Constantine, who prided himself on being a good judge of character, not only exonerated Athanasius, but excoriated Arius, the great foe of Athanasius, as a "criminal," whose "thinning hair, the pallor of his visage, his half-dead appearance—all . . . attest his vapidity and madness."[6] The emperor too could indulge in ill-tempered obloquy!

Arius went to Constantinople, the great new city Constantine had built as the capital of the empire, apologized to the emperor, and was forgiven by him. But the war within Christendom went on.

Attention and controversy continued to swirl around Athanasius, who became the main protagonist for the Nicene faction. By many accounts, he was a violent, ill-tempered man, who lashed out at his opponents with vitriolic abandon and behaved consistently in non-Christian ways toward others. He often acted more like a gangster than a Christian leader.

Though Athanasius clearly had unusual talent, he was a difficult and less than forthright man. One writer, Timothy Barnes, characterizes the man as follows: "In Alexandria itself, he maintained the popular support which he enjoyed from the outset and buttressed his position by organizing an ecclesiastical mafia. In later years, if he so desired, he could instigate a riot or prevent the orderly administration of the city. Athanasius possessed a power independent of the emperor which he built up and perpetuated by violence. That was both the strength and the weakness of his position. Like a modern gangster, he evoked widespread mistrust, proclaimed total innocence—and usually succeeded in evading conviction on specific charges."[7]

How, it may fairly be asked, can Christ's church be built on the leadership of such a slippery, violent character? And many of his Arian opponents were not much, if any, better! Leaders such as Athanasius illustrate how the church had become a human institution, a political entity with great power, part and parcel of the intrigue, back stabbing, obfuscation, and deceit characteristic of the imperial court.

The deadly game of ecclesiastical ping-pong went on for several decades, with first one side and then the other gaining temporary favor with the emperor of the day. It was no-holds-barred warfare, whose object was to gain and retain power, while crushing adversaries, using whatever tactics were considered necessary. Both sides engaged in despicable practices, acting more like street gangs than Christians.

As charges and countercharges continued to swirl around Athanasius, Constantine ordered a council of bishops to meet at Tyre, to consider charges against that violent and vengeful man—charges that ranged from assault, arson, and kidnapping to murder itself. (The latter charge clearly was trumped up or at least exaggerated by the Arians.) Athanasius, under threat from the emperor, reluctantly attended. After stormy debate, Athanasius was condemned for acts of violence and disobedience. He was excommunicated and ordered not to return to Alexandria, where he had been bishop. Athanasius appealed to Constantine for redress. At the hearing before the emperor, the Arians, led by Eusebius of Nicodemia, played their trump card. Athanasius, they claimed, had threatened to use his power to cut off shipments of grain from Alexandria to other ports within the empire.[8] This was a serious charge, and all concerned knew it. Squabbles about esoteric doctrinal differences were one thing, but threatening the peace and well-being of the empire by cutting off shipments of essential grain simply could not be tolerated. Constantine, furious, exiled Athanasius to a remote area on the German frontier. There, the bishop schemed and planned for his return. The war was not over, not by a long shot.

Arius, Athanasius's great rival, eventually was readmitted to the church by the *fourth* council, which had pronounced his theology to be orthodox and fully acceptable. (Readers will no doubt recall Arius and his teachings had been denounced by the Council of Nicea.) But Athanasius's allies refused to permit Arius to be readmitted to full communion, one of them declaring he would never deal with "the inventor of heresy."[9]

Then the Athanasians had a great stroke of luck, if that is what it was. Arius, the night before he was to receive communion, suffered a violent, agonizing stomachache and died within a few minutes.[10] Was it disease or poison? We will never know, but the stench of skullduggery still hangs over the whole affair. Certainly, Athanasius gloated over the death of his hated rival, comparing it to the death of Judas Iscariot.

Then Constantine died on 22 May A.D. 337, and for a time Roman unity was challenged, as Constantine's three sons fought for primacy. In the bloodbath that ensued, religious differences were for a time put on the back burner. Athanasius returned to Alexandria, where, so his enemies said, "he seized the churches . . . by force, by murder, by war."[11] Riots between Athanasius's supporters and the Arians tore Alexandria and other Eastern cities apart for several months. Finally, the new ruler in the East, Constantius, an Arian and son of Constantine, forcibly evicted Athanasius and several other prominent anti-Arian bishops, and exiled them to the West.

Unfortunately, all this accomplished in the long run was to pit the Western and Eastern churches against each other and begin a process that ended so tragically seven centuries later. More church councils failed to settle things down, and the Eastern and Western churches nearly split apart. A temporary stalemate occurred: the mostly Arian East, under Constantius, remained in uneasy and distrustful relationship with the anti-Arian West, under its Emperor Constans the brother of Constantius. But not for long: another council meeting in Antioch again condemned and deposed Athanasius, focusing not on his theology but on his violent acts and political chicanery.

Eventually, Constantius won his military and political battles and presided over the whole empire. With that power, he imposed religious unity, in effect undoing the anti-Arian decisions of the Council of Nicea. The Creed of Rimini-Seleucia substituted a simple, broadly inclusive statement of faith for the (to many) divisive Nicene Creed.

But enmity, bitterness, intrigue, deception, and bad faith still prevailed throughout Christendom. Athanasius continued to plot and scheme. Constantius died (perhaps from malaria), to be succeeded by Julian, the nephew of Constantine. Julian, who became known as "Julian the Apostate," turned his back on Christianity, embraced Neoplatonism, and aggressively promoted paganism by every means short of overt persecution. He was killed by a spear thrust in A.D. 363 during a battle with the Persians; rumor has it that his killer was one of his own Christian soldiers.[12]

The violence and killing between rival Christian groups continued. These often were extremely bloody affairs, as the following example illustrates. Five decades after the Council of Nicea, with Constantine long since in his grave, Damasus, the pope who commissioned Jerome to prepare the Vulgate edition of the Bible, was elected to his office as bishop of Rome after bitter struggles with a rival, Ursinus. Even by fourth-century standards, it was a bloody fracas, with more than 160 dead bodies of men and women discovered in one basilica alone. Jesus' admonition to "love your enemies, bless them that curse you, do good to them that hate you, and pray for them that despitefully use you, and persecute you" (Matthew 5:44) had fallen on deaf ears!

Damasus soon gave refuge to Peter, a pro-Nicene cleric selected by Athanasius to replace him as bishop of Alexandria, but rejected by the emperor, Valens, who had Arian leanings. An Arian bishop, Lucius, was installed, with the armed support of imperial troops. Unholy alliances between the secular and

ecclesiastical powers were, of course, commonplace. Soon after-
wards, Valens, the pro-Arian emperor, was slaughtered, along
with most of the Roman Army of the East, in a terrible battle
with the Goths. (The Goths were a nomadic people from beyond
the eastern frontiers of the empire, whose love of war was legendary.) It was the worst defeat in the history of Roman arms,
and to many superstitious folk seemed to symbolize God's anger
at the Arians and His judgment on them. God, said the Niceans,
finally had chosen sides, and the Arians were the losers.

From then on, the Arian cause fell into steep decline, at least
in the Western church. Many Christians, both laity and clergy,
were deeply worried about the pressures on the frontiers of the
empire from invading Huns and Goths. They wanted an all-
powerful Jesus—the Jesus of the Nicene Creed—who would res-
cue them from earthly woes, protect them from their enemies,
and was no less mighty than God the Father. If heads had to be
broken to secure that point of view or theological differences
abandoned or at least submerged, so be it.

Theodosius, the emperor who succeeded the hapless Valens,
saw himself as the defender of orthodoxy, the enemy of the
Arians, the scourge of unbelievers. In A.D. 380, Theodosius
began to put his principles into practice. Arian bishops, he proclaimed, could either accept the Nicene Creed or go into exile.
All the inhabitants of the empire were to follow "the form of
religion handed down by the apostle Peter to the Romans." All
other teaching was considered "heretical poison," and was to be
abandoned forthwith.[13]

The Council of Constantinople, held in A.D. 381, with only
Eastern bishops attending, adopted a creed of belief—essentially
the Nicene Creed with a few minor variations—and affirmed the
orthodox Christian belief in "one holy Catholic and apostolic
Church." Western bishops soon followed suit. The Arian cause,
though it hung around for a while in the East, was in irreversible

decline. By the seventh century, Arianism was no longer a major force, at least in the West.

Theodosius proclaimed Nicene Christianity to be the official, and only acceptable, religion of the Roman Empire. The movement begun by Constantine and the Nicene Council finally had reached its conclusion. The Father and Son, so orthodoxy proclaimed, were equal in all things, including their very substance.

Although Theodosius had declared orthodox Christianity to be the official religion of the empire, old pagan ways died hard. When Julian "The Apostate" emperor had arrived in Antioch in A.D. 362 on his way to fight the Persians, he found, to his intense annoyance even though he was pagan, there was no one there to greet him. The whole city, he found, was in mourning, bewailing the falsely believed annual death and resurrection of Adonis, the lover of Venus, the Roman expression of the Greek goddess Aphrodite.[14] Superstition and idolatrous worship of the pagan gods still remained a potent force nearly half a century after the heady days of the Nicene Council.

In an even more bizarre turn of events, in the fifth century, the pope had to stop the morning congregation at St. Peter's in Rome from walking up the church steps backwards so as not to offend Sol, the God of the rising sun.[15] "Sol's day" became Sunday, the Christian Sabbath. Christianity, though the official religion, was not even skin deep with many: the old gods of imperial Rome still lurked in the shadows.

Though for most Christians the question of the relationship between the Father and Son was settled for practical purposes at Constantinople in A.D. 381, doctrinal differences between the Eastern (Greek) and Western (Roman, or Latin) churches continued to plague Christendom. Western bishops objected strongly to the contention in the Niceno-Constantinopolitan creed that the Holy Spirit "proceedeth from the Father."[16] They insisted on adding the words "and the Son," so that the phrase describes the Holy Ghost as He who "proceedeth from the Father and the Son." This additional clause, known as the *Filoque,* was recited as part of the Catholic Mass in Western churches by the ninth century A.D. It became a major area of dispute between the Roman Catholic and Orthodox churches and played a significant role in the growing separation between Eastern and Western orthodoxy. Indeed, it is safe to say that to the Eastern church the dispute over what came to be known as the Double Procession of the Holy Ghost became the cornerstone of its quarrel with its Western counterpart. It was the vilest of heresies, so the Eastern church contended, to assert that the Holy Ghost proceeded from the Father and the Son.

Underlying this dispute was the lingering concern of Eastern churches, which just wouldn't go away, about the relationship between the Father and the Son. Eastern churches continued to believe that in some ways God the Father is different from God the Son. Western churches, on the other hand, were of equally strong belief that the Father and Son are of the same essence (homoousian) and hence equal in all things.

Over the years, various strongly held differences of opinion, centered on the perennial controversy over the nature of Christ, bedeviled the Eastern church. The Western churches, which thought the issue had been settled once for all time at Nicea, largely were indifferent to it. But in the Eastern churches, conciliar decrees that Jesus Christ was both human and divine, in effect one person with two natures, were not accepted by many church leaders. Eastern bishops rallied around the banner of belief in Christ's Single Nature, a doctrine known as monophysticism. Two centuries later, in the seventh century, Patriarch Sergius, one of the Eastern Patriarchs, attempted to solve the difference of opinion between the Eastern and Western churches. Sergius proposed that Christ, while possessing two natures, human and divine (as the Western churches believed), had only a single will and that was divine, not human. This doctrine, called monothelitism, the Doctrine of the Single Will, was agreed by all four Eastern Patriarchs. But in A.D. 641, the Western churches, whose spokesman was Pope John IV, flatly condemned the whole concept. A major schism loomed between East and West, and the two parts of Christendom drew even further apart.

Greek and Roman Christians found themselves increasingly separated not only by religious issues but also by social and cultural differences between East and West. Each side began to hold the other in contempt. The Romans felt the Greeks were effeminate fops; the Greeks averred that the Romans were uncouth, uncivilized, and illiterate semi-barbarians.

A rupture between the Eastern and Western churches became almost inevitable as a result of events that happened as the eighth century gave way to the ninth. The supreme ruler of the empire at the time was a woman named Irene, a beautiful but particularly odious creature thoroughly detested by her subjects, in part (but only in part) because she had ordered the brutal murder of her son, the Emperor Constantine VI. While Irene connived and schemed in Constantinople, in Western Europe a new secular power, that of the Franks, was rising. On Christmas day in A.D. 800, at St. Peter's in Rome, Pope Leo III crowned the king of the Franks, Charles, with the title Emperor of the Romans. So far as both Charles and Leo were concerned, the throne of the emperors was unoccupied. Whatever her virtues, or lack of them, Irene was in their eyes a usurper, debarred from senior leadership by her gender. Women, Western tradition falsely averred, simply were incapable of governance.

Charles, known to history as Charlemagne, went on to be a brilliant ruler, superb statesman, and patron of the so-called Carolingian Renaissance that reawakened Western Europe. To that extent the pope, by giving Charles a leg up, did him a great favor. But Leo did the papacy a much greater favor, by demonstrating that the pope, and he alone, had the power to confer the imperial crown as his personal gift, with all that implied about papal superiority and seniority over whomever he invested with power. That purported right arose from the infamous *Donation of Constantine,* termed by one well-known historian as the "best-known forgery in history."[17] Sometime in the eighth century, perhaps about A.D. 750, someone in the papal chancery (records office) in Rome prepared a forged document, which stated that Constantine the Great had been cured of leprosy by the pope back in the fourth century. In gratitude, the bogus story went on, Constantine gave his imperial crown and all its power to the then bishop of Rome (supposedly Pope Sylvester) and made him (and by extension his successors) head of all the priests in the Roman world. Sylvester, so the legend said, generously and out of the goodness of his heart restored the crown to Constantine, as a gift. The moral of the story is obvious: the pope is the supreme authority in Christendom. Crowns are his to give or take back. He makes and breaks monarchs. Above kings and emperors, he can do as he pleases in both temporal and spiritual realms. The story was widely considered to be true in medieval Christendom, and was only shown to be a blatant forgery in the fifteenth century by the scholar Lorenzo Valla, who endured the furious wrath of the papal office to tell the truth. But underlying it was the arrogant assumption that the Roman bishop could do whatever he chose, both ecclesiastically and secularly.

The Byzantines were both appalled and enraged by Leo's actions in crowning Charlemagne. The unthinkable had occurred. What arrogance, they thought, that a jumped-up, boorish, illiterate Frank should ever consider himself fit to wear the crown of Constantine the Great. And what was the Bishop of Rome up to, assuming that he, and he alone, could decide who would be emperor of the Romans? It was against the order of heaven, foul sacrilege, to say the least. They rejected the actions of both Charles and Leo, while recognizing that the centuries-old dream of a united Christian empire was dying. Henceforth, there would be two empires, not one. Christendom was fractured, the old order gone forever.[18]

The increasing separation and open hostility between East and West culminated in June of A.D. 1054, when Pope Leo IX's representatives in Constantinople excommunicated the Greek Patriarch. He and the other Eastern patriarchs could play the same game: they promptly excommunicated the Roman Catholic church.[19] Christendom was split asunder. How far the church had drifted from its apostolic moorings!

The celebrated French medievalist, Jacques Le Goff, has noted that by the eleventh century A.D. the papacy had "proclaimed itself to be the head of the lay as well as of the religious hierarchy. From there it strove to make the subordination of imperial and royal power to its own power obvious and effective. . . . The secular arm [i.e., the royal power], carried out the commands of the priestly order, and polluted itself in the place of the Church by using physical force and violence and spilling the blood of which the Church washed its hands."[20]

The arrogance of power is further illustrated by an episode in the tenure of Pope Gregory VII, who ascended to his office in A.D. 1073. Gregory published soon thereafter a disturbing statement of papal power, under the heading *Dictatus Papae*. Norman Cantor outlines its contents:

"The *Dictatus Papae* asserted that the Roman church was founded by God alone; that only the papal office was universal in its authority; and that the pope alone could depose bishops, reinstate them, or transfer them from one see to another. No church council was canonical without papal approval. No one could condemn an appellant to the apostolic see, which was the supreme court of Christendom. No decree or book was to be considered canonical without papal assent. Furthermore, the pope was said to be beyond the judgment of any human being; his actions were to be judged by God alone. The Roman church, by which is presumably meant the papacy, had never erred, and according to the Scriptures it never would err. The Roman pontiff was sanctified by the merits of St. Peter. No one could be a true Catholic unless he agreed with the pope. A final group of propositions in the *Dictatus Papae* dealt with church-state relations. It was asserted that only the pope could use the imperial insignia, implying that the pope was the true successor to Constantine. The pope had the power to depose emperors, and it was lawful for subjects to bring accusations against their rulers to the papal see."[21]

Lord Acton was right: "Power tends to corrupt and absolute power corrupts absolutely."[22] Incidentally, as the Catholic writer Garry Wills has noted, Acton was "speaking of papal absolutism—more specifically, he was condemning a fellow historian's book on Renaissance Popes for letting them literally get away with murder."[23]

Marcus Aurelius, the good and wise man who served (A.D. 161–180) as the last of the "five good emperors," penned much the same thought as that expressed by Lord Acton. He concluded that "malice, craftiness, and duplicity are the concomitants of absolute power."[24]

The years after the Council of Nicea show clearly that the church, by becoming entangled with the power politics of the imperial court, by failing to "render unto Caesar the things which are Caesar's; and unto God the things that are God's," in Jesus' famous words (Matthew 22:21), became a powerful human institution, an instrument of state policy, or more often a rival thereof. True, it retained a form of piety and exerted tremendous power, but it had long since lost all legitimate claim to be called Christ's church. Violence, murder, abuse of power, avarice, licentiousness, deceit, and all the other vices displayed by "orthodox" church leaders over the years have no place in the kingdom of God.

NOTES

1. Quoted in Johnson, *A History of Christianity*, 77.
2. See chapter 4, note 27, of this book.
3. Quoted in Johnson, *A History of Christianity*, 79.
4. Rubenstein, *When Jesus Became God*, 101.
5. See ibid., 108–25.
6. Quoted in ibid., 114.
7. Barnes, *Constantine and Eusebius*, 230.
8. See Rubenstein, *When Jesus Became God*, 128–30.
9. Quoted in ibid., 135.
10. See ibid., 135–36.
11. Quoted in ibid., 142.
12. See ibid., 201.
13. Frend, *The Rise of Christianity*, 636; see also *Documents of the Christian Church*, 22.
14. See Romer, *Testament*, 230.
15. See ibid., 231.
16. *Documents of the Christian Church*, 26.
17. Cantor, *The Civilization of the Middle Ages*, 176; see also 177–78.
18. See Norwich, *A Short History of Byzantium*, 109–20.
19. See *Documents of the Christian Church*, 97.
20. Le Goff, *Medieval Civilization 400–1500*, 271.
21. Cantor, *Civilization of the Middle Ages*, 258.
22. *The Oxford Dictionary of Quotations*, 1.
23. Wills, *Papal Sin*, 2.
24. Aurelius, *Meditations*, 7.

CHAPTER EIGHT

HERESY AND HERETICS

A S COULD BE EXPECTED, GIVEN the already corroding and spreading influences of apostasy and the existence of hundreds of pagan cults of every sort, it was not long before grievous heresies began to plague and further tear apart the infant church. Indeed, it is safe to say that during its first three centuries, at least, the Christian church was fragmented and diverse. Such lack of unity and diversity of both doctrine and practices sapped strength from the church and drew public attention and hence hostility (at least potentially) toward all Christians. There were many dozens of heretical movements, grouped around charismatic leaders, each claiming to have divine authority. Some of the most important include the following:

THE GNOSTICS

The word *Gnostic* comes from the Greek *gnōsis* (knowledge). The Gnostics, and there were many varieties of them, believed that only a few chosen ones had access to secret knowledge about the nature of God and the origin and destiny of humankind. The source of this special knowledge, it was claimed, was either the original Apostles, from whom it had been obtained by some sort of secret tradition, or by direct revelation given by God Himself to the founder of the movement. Some Gnostic teachings incorporate philosophical speculation of the Neoplatonic type, but others represent "wild amalgams of mythology and magical rites drawn from all quarters, with the most slender admixture of Christian elements."[1]

Gnosticism was a serious and substantial threat to the early church, in essence a rival for men's hearts and minds. By the end of the second century it had infected, in one form or another, almost all "intellectual" Christian congregations. The combination of special knowledge, elitism, and secrecy were alluringly seductive to many. Since most Christian congregations by that time contained large percentages of Hellenized ex-Gentiles, heavily influenced by Greek philosophy, there were but few Christian groups, we can be sure, in which Gnosticism did not sing its siren song.

One of the characteristics of Gnostic teaching was that the physical world is evil and antagonistic to the spiritual; matter itself is wicked and corrupt; and the human body also is evil. To Gnostics, salvation comes only by overcoming and eliminating the material environment—the wicked world in all its aspects—through "gnosis" and the secret rites associated with it. The belief that the body and the world itself are evil tended to lead Gnostics into one or the other of two extreme positions: asceticism, which denied the body has legitimate physical needs, or licentiousness, which claimed that since the body is evil anyway, sexual promiscuity is of no concern to either God or man.

Gnostics thought that because the physical world is intrinsically and completely wicked, God could not have created it. To their twisted way of thinking, some lesser being, an inferior deity, whom they called the "demiurge," had done so. The word *demiurge* was used by Plato in his description of the formation of the physical world. The admixture of Platonic thought with debased Christian doctrine was seductively appealing to Hellenized peoples.

Gnostics believed that Christ came to earth as an emissary of the supreme God, bringing "gnosis" to a select few, but that he could not have soiled Himself in a physical body. That led to a major problem for the Gnostics: how does one explain the presence of the earthly Jesus? Two major attempts were made to deal with the issue, each more ludicrous than the other. They were as follows:

DOCETISM

The word comes from the Greek *dokio,* meaning "I seem," or "to seem to be." Docetism proclaimed that the humanity and suffering of the earthly Christ were apparent rather than real. Christ, they asserted, only *appeared* to be the man Jesus. The physical body Christ displayed after the resurrection thus was only illusory, not real; a phantom, not flesh and bones.[2]

Other variations of Docetism had Christ escaping death by having someone else take his place on the cross—perhaps Judas Iscariot or Simon the Cyrene, who carried Christ's cross. Jesus, it was said, "took on the appearance of Simon and stood by and mocked them."[3]

This nonsense flies in the face of the scriptural record and of Jesus' own account of His suffering as recorded in latter-day revelation (see D&C 19:16–19). And what it says about Jesus is unspeakable.

CERINTHIANISM

The other major attempt by Gnostics to explain away the earthly life of Jesus is called Cerinthianism, named after Cerinthus, its chief proponent in the first century A.D. The

Cerinthians taught that Jesus, though He began life as a mere mortal, was changed at His baptism by a higher Divine power, which descended upon Him.[4] That power, Cerinthus argued, left Jesus just before His suffering on the cross. If this be true, the divine Christ did not die for our sins; it was only the man Jesus who did so.

Despite strenuous efforts by church leaders to counteract this devilish and dangerous heresy, it took its toll. Irenaeus (circa A.D. 130–200), the celebrated bishop of Lyons, recounts how John the Beloved Apostle "went to the baths at Ephesus; and rushed out, without taking a bath, when he saw Cerinthus inside, exclaiming, 'Let us get away before the baths fall in; for Cerinthus is in there, the enemy of the truth.'"[5]

As an aside, it is interesting to note that Irenaeus "attributed the appearances of God in the Old Testament to his Son [as Latter-day Saints do], 'showing God to man in many ways lest man wholly lacking God, should cease to exist.' Human being, therefore, was not the result of creation by an inferior God or by evilly disposed powers, but was made by God, through divine benevolence and for a set purpose."[6]

Marcion, whom some have termed the "arch heretic," or as Polycarp called him, "Satan's eldest son,"[7] was Docetic in some of his teachings. Born about A.D. 85 at a place called Sinope, on the south shore of the Black Sea, he inherited a fortune from his father, a wealthy ship owner and reputedly bishop of the town at a time when there were no paid clergy. Marcion taught that the earth was created by an inferior being, the demiurge, and rejected completely the Old Testament and its God, whom he claimed to be capricious, monstrous, and wicked. Christianity, he said, was not a continuation of the Old Testament religion of the Jews but a completely new revelation.[8] Scripture, Marcion believed, could not be understood allegorically. It had to be accepted or rejected on its factual merits. Marcion considered that only the Apostle

Paul understood the essential difference between the Christian gospel—the gospel of love; and the Jewish scripture—the Law of Moses. Others of the apostles, he stated (in error), had been blinded to the truth by Jewish influences. Accordingly, he believed the Christians should establish their own canon of scripture, which he indicated should consist of only seven of the Pauline epistles and a shortened version of Luke's gospel.[9] Paul, Marcion believed, was the actual author of Luke's gospel; someone, he said, had added Old Testament material to Paul's writings. Hence the need, so Marcion thought, to delete parts of what we know as Luke's gospel.

Marcion also taught the need for baptism for the dead, in conformity with Paul's teachings (see 1 Corinthians 15:29).[10] For this, he was accused of heresy, and condemned by "orthodox" Christians. But on this doctrinal issue, Marcion was correct, though it would take until 1840 for this truth to be restored by the Prophet Joseph Smith.[11] Doctrinal purity already was slipping away from the early church.

Marcion's insistence on the need for a uniquely Christian canon of scripture undoubtedly hastened the day when "orthodox" Christians compiled such a work, with all the difficulties and uncertainties associated with that endeavor.

Marcion was a vigorous personality and excellent organizer. He insisted his adherents follow a strict moral code and tried to make his own personal life conform to the teachings and example of Jesus as he understood them.

Marcion was excommunicated in A.D. 144 but continued his efforts to organize his own church. At that he was spectacularly successful, such that it has been stated that "his followers were certainly the chief danger to the Church from dogmatic unorthodoxy in the latter half of the 2nd cent."[12]

MONTANISM

An important apocalyptic movement of the latter half of the second century A.D. can be traced to a man named Montanus, who lived in Phrygia, a region of inland Asia Minor. Montanus proclaimed that the second coming of the Savior was near at hand and that the church would have to be purified and reformed before His return.[13] In response to Montanus's description of the very place to which he believed the heavenly Jerusalem would descend (a desert locale), people abandoned homes, families, and work and gathered in solemn anticipation at the sacred place. Alas, the prophesied event did not materialize, but the Montanist movement only grew in strength.

Montanus was, so he said, himself a prophet. Two women closely associated with him, Prisca (or Priscilla) and Maximilla, proclaimed Montanus to be the embodiment of the Holy Ghost. And his followers believed that to be so.[14]

Montanus understood that the church had departed from its apostolic moorings and had to return to the basic teachings of first-century Christianity. In that he was correct, but he evidently failed to realize that priesthood authority to direct and control necessary changes had already been lost.

Montanism spread very rapidly—in Asia Minor, Greece, North Africa—even as far as Gaul. One of its great attractions was Montanus's insistence on moral worthiness among Christians. "The Montanists were," says one authority, "evidently sincere, holy and probably humble and abstemious people."[15]

Montanus recognized that in contrast to its beginnings, the church had, by his time, grown lax in its moral standards. Gross immorality, which, he said, had led to excommunication in earlier days, now resulted only in a rap on the knuckles and a promise by the sinner to reform. Montanus would not allow persons who had recanted their Christian beliefs during persecution to be rebaptized. He forbade divorce and refused to allow second marriages. Absolute honesty was required in the business and personal lives of church members, and merchants were not allowed to engage in businesses that profited from idolatry.[16]

The response of "orthodox" church leaders to Montanus was what one would expect from an organization that had gone so far astray: "Let bygones be bygones," they said of lapsed members. "Just forget the past. Times have changed, and standards of behavior have to change with them." Montanus was condemned by an increasingly secularized and institutionalized church. It is, however, interesting that Tertullian, who had begun as a severe critic of Montanism and was widely known as the scourge of heretics, joined the Montanist movement toward the end of his life. He could no longer endorse an orthodoxy that denied the role of the Holy Ghost and claimed that all communication with God had to be through the clergy. Tertullian could not accept the increasing worldliness of the church and its spiritual barrenness. One authority describes Tertullian's embrace of Montanism as follows: "Here was a great Church statesman, a man of impeccable rectitude and burning faith, embracing heresy. His adherence thus completely undermines the orthodox attacks on the morals and public behaviour of the Montanists, sets a stamp of ethical approval, at any rate, on the movement."[17] Montanism was still vigorous until the sixth century, and survived until at least the eighth century A.D.

MANICHEISM

Manes, or Mani, as he also is known, evidently was born in Mesopotamia, about A.D. 215. Little is known about his life, but he reportedly spent time in India, learning Eastern religious thought. His teachings, supported by a formidable missionary force, were widespread by the end of the third century A.D. in

Rome, Egypt, and elsewhere. Mani taught a peculiar mélange of beliefs, most of them not even Christian, though he proclaimed that the truths and secrets he embraced were the principles of Gnosticism brought together and revealed to the world. To Mani, the purpose of religion was to release the particles of Light that Darkness had stolen, and which were "trapped in evil matter, the trees, the earth and all living creatures."[18] Plato, Moses, Jesus, Zoroaster, Buddha, and Mani himself, so he proclaimed, had been sent to earth to help in this task. Mani believed he could integrate all human religious experiences into a single, universal system. Or so he claimed, and many believed him.

The Manicheans were secretive and aloof, with "underground" networks which kept them in touch with each other. Their pessimistic views about human potential were balanced by their equally passionate belief in a godly elite. They preached the value of asceticism and practiced scrupulous vegetarianism. The true Manichean lived on "light-bearing" vegetables, such as melons and others "of concentrated goodness."[19] They did no work, which only delayed the triumph of light. All governments, Christian, Zoroastrian, Roman, or Persian, hated and despised the Manicheans, and most persecuted them. Mani himself reportedly was flayed alive at Persian government orders.

Augustine, the fifth-century bishop who is considered the greatest of the so-called Christian Fathers, was in his youth a Manichean, before he became Christian.[20] Some believe that Augustine's unusual views on sex were the result of his Manichean training.

THE EBIONITES

The Ebionites take their name not from a man named Ebion, but from a Hebrew word meaning "poor men." The Ebionites were a sect of Jewish-Christians, whose name in Hebrew probably derives from the fact that many of the Jerusalem Saints often were in temporal need. Soon after Paul's conversion, he was called by Barnabas to Antioch, where the two were sent with "relief unto the brethren which dwelt in Judea" (Acts 11:29). Paul continued his charitable activities: after his third mission he admonished the Saints in Galatia and in Corinth to provide generously, that he might send designated messengers "to bring your liberality unto Jerusalem" (Acts 16:3). Church members in Macedonia had given liberally out of "deep poverty" (2 Corinthians 8:1–2), and Paul expected the Saints in Corinth to give liberally and cheerfully out of their "abundance" (2 Corinthians 8:14). God, Paul knew, "loveth a cheerful giver" (2 Corinthians 9:7).

The Jerusalem Saints at this time were in the main Jewish-Christians. It was not long before they began to receive persecution from the Jews (see 1 Thessalonians 2:14–15). By A.D. 85, the liturgy of the synagogue in Jerusalem included this phrase: "May the Nazarenes [i.e., the Jewish-Christians] and the heretics be suddenly destroyed and removed from the Book of Life."[21]

Given the divergence of ways in which the two religious groups were developing, a break between Judaism and Christianity was inevitable. As the number of gentile converts grew from a trickle to a flood, Jewish-Christians began to feel more estranged from the mainstream of Christianity. They continued to observe Jewish feasts and to require circumcision. Some of them were agnostic at best about the virgin birth of Jesus,[22] and in general believed Him to be the mortal son of Mary and Joseph, upon whom the Holy Spirit had descended at baptism. Jewish-Christians continued to believe in the binding nature of the Mosaic Law. Mainstream Christianity had moved on to an understanding that the Mosaic Law, so dear to Jewish hearts, had been a "schoolmaster *to bring us unto Christ*" (Galatians 3:24).

The Jewish-Christians became lonely, estranged, and

embittered, left behind in the often chaotic world of religious change. Irenaeus lumped them in with other heretical groups. Though there were still small groups of Jewish-Christians in Syria in the fourth century, they were supported neither by the Jews, who could not forgive them for being Christians, nor by the Christians, who were dismayed and no doubt insulted by their continued observance of Jewish rites and customs. They became irrelevant to both Jews and Christians, and faded out of history.

THE VALENTINIANS

Perhaps the most influential of the Gnostics was a man named Valentinus, who lived in the second century A.D. and spent most of his life in Rome, where he was nearly chosen as bishop (probably about A.D. 143). His followers claimed Valentinus had been educated in Egypt by a pupil of the Apostle Paul, but that is not provable at this date. By all accounts he had an outstanding intellect and was widely respected as a teacher. Valentinus was a Platonist, who believed, as did other Gnostics, in Hellenized portions of Christian doctrine. He rejected the basic Christian belief that Jesus was the incarnation of God, and proposed, as did the Docetics, that the divine Christ was pure spirit and that Jesus' physical appearance was merely an illusion.[23] The earth, indeed the entire universe, had been formed not by the utterly unknowable God, but by an inferior deity. Valentinus believed that only the elect, those who were Gnostic initiates in possession of special, secret knowledge, were certain of salvation. Ordinary church members, with faith but no "gnosis," might *perhaps* receive *some* degree of salvation; but the heathens, engrossed in things material, were completely bereft of all hope and damned forever. What is worse, the three categories were predetermined from eternity.

Valentinus claimed that the mysteries of Gnosticism, the

special knowledge it possessed, had been taught by Jesus to His apostles and passed on by them to a select few.[24]

Several of Valentinus's pupils became important Gnostic teachers, contributing significantly to the spread of Gnosticism in Alexandria, Italy, and Gaul, during the last years of the second century.[25]

Irenaeus railed against the followers of Valentinus, whom he called guilty of "insolent blasphemy against their Creator."[26] Valentinus's teachings were easily considered as orthodox by people who did not understand their subtle distortions. Though seen by many as faithful Christians, the Valentinians actually subverted the faith and were in reality wolves in sheep's clothing. They deserved, Irenaeus believed correctly, to be cut off from Christian fellowship.[27]

Heresies came and went, each of them drawing people away from the simple truths of Christ's gospel and reflecting a lack of strong, divinely authorized leadership in the church. Beginning with Constantine, the "orthodox" church, aided by the secular power, persecuted those who did not agree with it, driving them underground or killing them if that seemed the only way to deal with them. Orthodoxy would be enforced, with the sword if need be. Thus, Theodosius, protector of the orthodox and sworn enemy of heresy, in his edicts of A.D. 380–381 prescribed the following fate for heretics:

"It is our desire that all the various nations which are subject to our Clemency and Moderation, should continue in the profession of that religion which was delivered to the Romans by the divine Apostle Peter, as it hath been preserved by faithful tradition; and which is now professed by the Pontiff Damasus and by Peter, Bishop of Alexandria, a man of apostolic holiness. According to the apostolic teaching and the doctrine of the Gospel, let us believe the one deity of the Father, the Son and the Holy Spirit, in equal majesty and in a holy Trinity. We authorize the followers of this law to assume the title of Catholic Christians; but as for the others, since, in our judgment, they are foolish madmen, we decree that they shall be branded with the ignominious name of heretics, and shall not presume to give to their conventicles the name of churches. They will suffer in the first place the chastisement of the divine condemnation, and in the second the punishment which our authority, in accordance with the will of Heaven, shall decide to inflict.

" . . . Let them be entirely excluded even from the thresholds of churches, since we permit no heretics to hold their unlawful assemblies in the towns. If they attempt any disturbance, we decree that their fury shall be suppressed and that they shall be expelled outside the walls of the cities, so that the Catholic churches throughout the world may be restored to the orthodox bishops who hold the faith of Nicaea."[28]

Roman Catholic treatment of the so-called Albigensian heresy, ruthlessly suppressed in France from the eleventh to the thirteenth centuries, tells us much of the errors of a rigid orthodoxy convinced it could do no wrong.

The teachings of the Albigensians contained elements of Manicheism and Doceticism. There were, they said, two eternal principles, good and bad. All matter was bad. Spirits were created by the good principle, but when they fell from their goodness they became imprisoned in bodies as a punishment until they had expiated their guilt and merited heaven. Christ, so the Albigensians claimed, was an angel with a phantom body, sent to teach man the true Albigensian doctrine, but did not die or rise again.

Strange beliefs, to be sure. Despite that, however, the Albigensians, or Cathars as they also were known, lived lives of self-denial and peaceful toleration. Their teachings were widely received by people who contrasted the Albigensian way of life—pacifism, tolerance, and poverty—with the moral laxity of some

Catholic clergy and the worldliness of the established and all-powerful church.

The Roman Catholic Church, in one of the more sordid episodes in its history, ordered a crusade against the Albigensians. It was conducted with unsurpassed brutality and cruelty by troops commissioned by great French landowners responding to the pope's command. "Kill them all; God will know His own," became their battle cry. For example, at Béziers, a town in the southwest of France, 15,000 to 20,000 people were massacred in a single morning in the summer of A.D. 1209. Every living soul, Catholic and Cathar alike, from baby to greybeard, who could be found and cut down, was put to the sword, and the town burned. The head of the Cistercian order of monks, Arnold Amaury, a man without a scintilla of scruples, later awarded for his efforts by appointment as archbishop of Narbonne, wrote to Pope Innocent III: "The workings of divine vengeance have been wondrous."[29]

Within two centuries, what armed soldiery had begun the Inquisition finished. Stephen O'Shea, a skilled chronicler of the "revolutionary life and death of the medieval Cathars" in his book, *The Perfect Heresy,* tells us of those terrible years: "By the middle of the fourteenth century, the Inquisition had razed any residual trace of the Albigensian heresy from the landscape of Christendom, and the Cathars of Languedoc had vanished. The stations of their calvary—the mass burnings, blindings, and hangings, the catapulting of body parts over castle walls, the rapine, the looting, the chanting of monks behind battering rams, the secret trials, the exhuming of corpses, the creakings of the rack—match our phantasmagoria of the medieval only too well."[30] Incidentally, a leading Inquisitor was Bishop Jacques Fournier, who later became Pope Benedict XII.

Nor should it be thought that only the Western (Roman, or Latin) church was capable of such behavior. The Eastern church also was guilty of the shedding of much innocent blood. One example of the many that could be cited will make the point. In the seventeenth century, Patriarch Nikon of the Russian Orthodox church, in an attempt to purify and revitalize the church, proposed sweeping revisions in its liturgy and ritual. The common people, joined by the lower clergy, cried out in anguish. To them the old ways of their fathers were the keys to salvation. "Give us back our Christ," devoted believers cried.

A full-scale religious rebellion ensued. Those who refused to accept the reforms became known as the Old Believers. Soon they were opposed by both the Russian Orthodox Church and the state, who brought all their formidable resources to bear against those who would not give up their old ways. An estimated 20,000 Old Believers were burned to death in a six-year period between 1684 and 1690, preferring martyrdom to acceptance of what was to them the Antichrist.

Provincial governors were instructed to provide to Russian Orthodox Church leaders whatever troops were necessary to enforce the established religion. Those who did not attend church were questioned, and if suspected of heresy, were tortured. But despite torture, the state, and exile, the Old Believers did not disappear. Many fled to refuge in isolated northern communities on the fringe of Russian society. Peter the Great, a generation later, saw that the Old Believers were sober and industrious people. "Leave them alone," he instructed his officials.

The schism in the Russian Orthodox Church between reformers and those who clung to the old ways failed to purify it, as Nikon had hoped. The church exhausted its energies and was a "disorganized, lethargic body whose corruption, ignorance and superstition must be vigorously purged, becoming permanently subordinate to the power of the state."[31]

Finally, in any discussion of heresy and heretics, the point must be made that after the first few centuries of the Christian era, uninspired orthodoxy, in collaboration with the secular power, determined what was heresy. This having been done, no effort was spared to root out and destroy those who dared to go counter to the orthodox position. Change or innovation was violently rejected, and there was no tolerance for dissent. God had spoken, the heavens were closed, revelation was no more. Arrogant and uninspired men would make the decisions and guard their power with jealous zeal. It would take a revelatory restoration of truth and light to change things.

NOTES

1. *The Oxford Dictionary of the Christian Church*, 565.
2. See Frend, *The Rise of Christianity*, 138, 372, 386; Johnson, *A History of Christianity*, 45, 89.
3. *Documents of the Christian Church*, 36.
4. See *Oxford Dictionary of the Christian Church*, 258.
5. *The Early Christian Fathers*, 92.
6. Frend, *The Rise of Christianity*, 246.
7. *Early Christian Fathers*, 92.
8. See Fox, *Pagans and Christians*, 332.
9. See Johnson, *History of Christianity*, 46–47.
10. Lyon, *Apostasy to Restoration*, 114.
11. *History of the Church*, 4:424–25.
12. *Oxford Dictionary of the Christian Church*, 854.
13. See Frend, *The Rise of Christianity*, 255–56.
14. See Johnson, *History of Christianity*, 49–50; *Oxford Dictionary of the Christian Church*, 918–19.
15. Johnson, *History of Christianity*, 50.
16. See Lyon, *Apostasy to Restoration*, 99–100.
17. Johnson, *History of Christianity*, 50.
18. Fox, *Pagans and Christians*, 567.
19. Ibid.
20. See Johnson, *History of Christianity*, 113.
21. Chadwick, *The Early Church*, 21.
22. See ibid., 23.
23. See ibid., 37–38.
24. See ibid., 41.

25. See Frend, *The Rise of Christianity*, 207.
26. *Early Christian Fathers*, 90.
27. See Pagels, *Beyond Belief*, 157–58.
28. *Documents of the Christian Church*, 22.
29. O'Shea, *The Perfect Heresy*, 87.
30. Ibid., 7.
31. Massie, *Peter the Great*, 61–64.

CHAPTER NINE

CONCLUSIONS

WHAT CAN WE CONCLUDE FROM this brief and sketchy review of several centuries of tumult and trial, as Christianity spread from a tiny seed to become not only a religious movement but an agent, ally, or (at least in the Latin West) a frequent competitor of the state, jealously guarding and extending its power at every opportunity, worldly, opulent, and arrogant? Some facts are, I think, self-evident.

1. *An institutional apostasy occurred,* as the church, devoid of apostolic leadership and direction, lost its way in the darkness of the world and embraced doctrines and practices that changed it from a divine to a worldly institution. In the process, sacred covenants were broken, essential ordinances altered or forgotten, the authority of the priesthood lost, the holy scriptures tampered with, and divine approbation understandably withdrawn. The church retained a form of godliness, some truth, and many devoted members, but it had strayed from its apostolic roots.

Some of our Christian friends, while admitting that the church changed during the first few centuries, put it all down to growing pains and necessary response to changing circumstances.

With the Council of Nicea, they say, church doctrine, beliefs, and organization were standardized, and change was no longer needed or acceptable. God's church, they proclaim, was now in place. God had spoken, once and for all. There was no need for further revelation.

I reject that view, though I respect it. The changes that occurred in the church were too deep-seated, too irreversible, too profound, too opposed to Christ's gospel of love, to be excused as the innocent thrashings around of a growing baby. And if Jesus' admonition "By their fruits ye shall know them" (Matthew 7:20) be true, as it surely is, the histories of the established churches over the last two millennia give no reason for confidence that they are Christ's church or can fully be approved by Him. The cynical view that so-called "orthodox" Christianity "must be divine because it survives such scandalous representatives,"[1] while clever, is specious. It simply misses the point. Survival, even worldly power and acclaim, is not the same as divine approval.

In making this judgment, I hasten to reiterate: all Christian churches retain portions of the truth; all have members—and this is true throughout the centuries—who love Jesus Christ; whose personal goodness puts me to shame; and who try as best they can to live according to His standards. We owe a great debt of gratitude to faithful men and women, doing their best, who kept the lamps of civilization burning during the long centuries before the dawning of a brighter day burst forth in the Restoration.

2. *We do not have many of the details of what happened to the early church and probably never will know them.* The records simply are not available, and we cannot, therefore, say exactly when and under what circumstances the damaging changes were made. But we do know that there is a void in early church history—a kind of "black hole," if you will—and that the church

that went into the void, was much, much different from that which we glimpse on the other side.

3. *The damage was done early.* We need look no further than the first two centuries of the Christian era. They were the years, long before a "universal" Christian church can be identified, when mortal injury was inflicted on the church. If the Nephite experience is any guide, it doesn't take very long for an organization to slip into apostasy. The deliberations and conclusions of the Council of Nicea and those that followed it, therefore, are not the cause but the result of apostasy. Similarly, although Greek philosophy certainly did influence Christian theology, by the time it had done so, the church was already apostate. Greek thought did not cause the apostasy. It became integrated into an already apostate organization.

4. *Much of the damage resulted from mutiny, from internal dissent and contention.* It was, in a sense, self-inflicted. The early apostles understood that internal dissension would tear the church apart, and was in fact already doing so in their day. That is why they repeatedly warned the saints of the dangers of internecine warfare. The chilling though admittedly unsubstantiated possibility that Peter and Paul were betrayed to the Roman authorities by "false brethren" and subsequently murdered (see chapter 5) only underscores the disastrous effects internal dissension undoubtedly had on the early church.

How could the infant church, torn and riven by dissent, have the strength, constancy, and sense of destiny to withstand heretics and heretical movements, persecution, and perhaps most difficult, the seduction of power? Of course, it couldn't and didn't. Most importantly, priesthood authority soon was lost, as it always is when men exercise unrighteous dominion or give way to greed and worldly ambition. In the absence of that power, divine approbation for the church was withdrawn.

5. *Persecution played a role,* though I believe it had much less

of an impact than Christian traditions and popular mythology assert. Persecution was never empire-wide, even in the days of Diocletian, who wanted it to be so but was prevented from imposing his intent by bureaucratic inefficiency, corruption, and popular reluctance. It is well to keep in mind that if the Romans had really set their minds to it, they could have wiped the Christian church off the face of the earth during the first century, at least. The Romans were, after all, a formidable military machine, and their bloody-minded ferocity was well established, as witness, for example, the sack of Jerusalem less than four decades after Jesus' death.

Persecution brought out both the best and the worst in Christians. Some were prepared to die for the cause, and did so under horrifying circumstances, serving as examples of courage and faith for the ages. Many others, however, folded under pressure and recanted their beliefs. The collective and individual sense of guilt that must have been felt by those all-too-human individuals who were not prepared to die must have lain heavy on their shoulders and impeded both individual and institutional growth. And it caused a lot of grief for church leaders, who differed in what to do with the *traditores* (the betrayers).

6. *Something must have gone terribly wrong with the procedure for transferring divine power and authority.* After the death of the original apostles and the few others we know were later ordained to that office, the orderly and divinely sanctioned transmission of power and authority to other priesthood holders petered out.

If the same principles of priesthood government applied in the early church as are operative in the restored Church of Jesus Christ of Latter-day Saints (and this seems a reasonable assumption), we know from scripture and the words of the living prophets that the quorum of the Twelve Apostles is equal in authority to that of the First Presidency (see D&C 107). [2] The Quorum of the Twelve is authorized to direct the affairs of the

Church in all the world and to reorganize the First Presidency if the latter is dissolved by reason of the death of the President of the Church. Similarly, the Seventy has authority equal to that of the other two more senior quorums and has the power to reorganize the Twelve if the First Presidency and Twelve were all to die. That principle extends even further, such that if all the Seventy were to die, responsibility and authority to reorganize the Church would fall upon the standing high councils and ultimately on the last surviving faithful Mechizedek Priesthood bearer. Clearly something cataclysmic went wrong in the early church which prevented this from happening, though we do not know the details.

My guess—and it can only be a guess, given the passage of nearly twenty centuries since the events happened—is that whatever went wrong in priesthood government related to the extreme factionalism and dissension in the early church, the inexperience of local leaders, combined with the lack of continued central direction and control, and the tremendous difficulties of communication between senior leaders with general authority and the small, scattered local units of the church.

I shudder to think what might have happened to the restored Church—The Church of Jesus Christ of Latter-day Saints—had the Prophet Joseph Smith been killed during the Kirtland period, when there was a dangerous amount of local dissension. Praise be that didn't happen, and I for one discern the hand of the Lord in protecting His latter-day church from what could have been a disastrous repetition of the fate of the church established in the meridian of time.

Authority in the early church seems to have been assumed by bishops, who became the highest church authorities. Though it is claimed that the apostles themselves placed bishops in those positions, proof of that assertion is lacking. The office of bishop soon became monarchical, in that bishops, who lived and acted like kings and were appointed for life, chose and even ordained their successors. For many centuries, Catholic bishops have been ordained by other bishops, having been selected by them or by other senior clergy. Thus, the office has become self-perpetuating in much of the Christian world.

7. *Though institutional apostasy will not occur again, as we have been promised, individual apostasy remains as easy as ever.* This lesson must never be forgotten. The Prophet Joseph Smith understood it well from observing the spirit of apostasy that grew among the Saints in Kirtland, Ohio, in 1836. There had been a rich outpouring of the Spirit in the weeks before and after the completion of the Kirtland Temple in the spring of that year. Joseph Smith warned the people: "Brethren, for some time Satan has not had power to tempt you. Some have thought that there would be no more temptation. But the opposite will come; and unless you draw near to the Lord you will be overcome and apostatize."[3]

Under the spirit of apostasy some Church members in Kirtland became proud, greedy, contentious, and disobedient to the commandments. Some, becoming bitter, sought to destroy that which they once had accepted. Apostates openly claimed that the Prophet had fallen and tried to have others put in his place. Shades of ancient Corinth, Ephesus, Antioch, and Alexandria!

The Prophet wrote of that time: "It seemed as though all the powers of earth and hell were combining their influence in an especial manner to overthrow the Church at once. . . . The enemy abroad, and apostates in our midst, united in their schemes . . . and many became disaffected toward me as though I were the sole cause of those very evils I was most strenuously striving against."[4] Joseph Smith's anguish parallels that of Paul, who cried to Timothy, "All they which are in Asia be turned away from me" (2 Timothy 1:15). Anguished loneliness is, I fear, the daily lot of the prophets of God.

Joseph Smith understood well the importance of unity if the affairs of the kingdom are to be protected and advanced. Heber C. Kimball summarized the Prophet's views as follows: "I will give you a key which br. Joseph Smith used to give in Nauvoo. He said that the very step of apostasy commenced with losing confidence in the leaders of this church and kingdom, and that whenever you discerned that spirit you might know that it would lead the possessor of it on the road to apostasy."[5]

The Prophet, in a long letter to Oliver Granger, amplified his views on the importance of unity: "In order to conduct the affairs of the Kingdom in righteousness, it is all important that the most perfect harmony, kind feeling, good understanding, and confidence should exist in the hearts of all the brethren; and that true charity, love one towards another, should characterize all their proceedings. If there are any uncharitable feelings, any lack of confidence, then pride, arrogance and envy will soon be manifested; confusion must inevitably prevail, and the authorities of the Church set at naught. . . .

"If the Saints in Kirtland deem me unworthy of their prayers when they assemble together, and neglect to bear me up at the throne of heavenly grace, it is a strong and convincing proof to me that they have not the Spirit of God. If the revelations we have received are true, who is to lead the people? If the keys of the Kingdom have been committed to my hands, who shall open out the mysteries thereof?

"As long as my brethren stand by me and encourage me, I can combat the prejudices of the world, and can bear the contumely [harsh treatment] and abuse with joy; but when my brethren stand aloof, when they begin to faint, and endeavor to retard my progress and enterprise, then I feel to mourn, but am no less determined to prosecute my task, being confident that although my earthly friends may fail, and even turn against me, yet my heavenly Father will bear me off triumphant.

"However, I hope that even in Kirtland there are some who do not make a man an offender for a word, but are disposed to stand forth in defense of righteousness and truth, and attend to every duty enjoined upon them; and who will have wisdom to direct them against any movement or influence calculated to bring confusion and discord into the camp of Israel, and to discern between the spirit of truth and the spirit of error.

"It would be gratifying to my mind to see the Saints in Kirtland flourish, but [I] think the time is not yet come; and I assure you it never will until a different order of things be established and a different spirit manifested. When confidence is restored, when pride shall fall, and every aspiring mind be clothed with humility as with a garment, and selfishness give place to benevolence and charity, and a united determination to live by every word which proceedeth out of the mouth of the Lord is observable, then, and not till then, can peace, order and love prevail.

"It is in consequence of aspiring men that Kirtland has been forsaken. How frequently has your humble servant been envied in his office by such characters, who endeavored to raise themselves to power at his expense, and seeing it impossible to do so, resorted to foul slander and abuse, and other means to effect his overthrow. Such characters have ever been the first to cry out against the Presidency, and publish their faults and foibles to the four winds of heaven."[6]

The Prophet also issued this solemn warning, which stands as a rebuke and a caution to Church members in our day: "I will give you one of the *Keys* of the mysteries of the Kingdom. It is an eternal principle, that has existed with God from all eternity: That man who rises up to condemn others, finding fault with the Church, saying that they are out of the way, while he himself is righteous, then know assuredly, that that man is in the high road to apostasy; and if he does not repent, will apostatize, as God lives."[7]

In light of these prophetic statements, who can doubt the malignant power of disunity, backbiting, and contention to lead men and women away into apostasy? Nor can we, in light of the Prophet's words and the tendency of men to err, but acknowledge that internal contention was a major cause of the apostasy of the early church.

8. *The victors write the histories.* The "orthodox" church, by then itself an apostate organization, determined which scriptures would be considered as canonical and what their content would be, who was a heretic and who was not; which practices were "Christian" and which were not. Some of the tampering with the scriptures that we know to have occurred, was done under its aegis, though I believe the crucial damage occurred before orthodoxy was imposed with an iron hand. The "orthodox" church, aided and abetted by the secular power, and in alliance with it, closed off all dissent, silenced those who did not agree with it, killing them if considered necessary, and saw anything— ranging from anatomy to astronomy—which did not fit its predetermined model, as something to be suppressed. On the other hand, we can be grateful to the "orthodox" church for keeping out of the official canon many speculative, fanciful apocryphal writings.

9. *The heavens have again been opened.* Thank heaven that God in His mercy gave another revelatory restoration to His children. It all began on a spring day in 1820, in upstate New York, on what was then the American frontier. "Two Personages, whose brightness and glory defy all description," appeared to a farm boy who wanted to know which church was true and which he should join. One of them spoke to the boy Joseph Smith, calling him "by name, and said, pointing to the other—This is My Beloved Son. Hear Him!" In Joseph Smith's own words, that conversation went as follows: "I was [told] that I must join none of [the churches of the day], for they were all wrong; and the

Personage who addressed me [Jesus Christ] said that all their creeds were an abomination in his sight; that those professors were all corrupt; that: 'they draw near to me with their lips, but their hearts are far from me, they teach for doctrines the commandments of men, having a form of godliness, but they deny the power thereof'" (Joseph Smith–History 1:17, 19).

More was learned about the nature of God the Father and His Son Jesus Christ in that single supernal manifestation than in all the councils ever convened and all the creeds ever codified! The dawning of a brighter day was about to burst upon the earth. The dispensation of the fulness of times was about to commence. It would sweep away the errors and misunderstandings of nearly two millennia and replace them with the simple restorative and rejuvenating truths of Christ's gospel as He and His apostles had preached it. Priesthood authority—the power to act in the name of God, to administer saving ordinances, and to bind on earth and have the act ratified in the heavens—would be restored to the earth, and the ancient government of Christ's church would again be reestablished. Sacred ordinances would be restored, along with the ancient covenants associated with them. In short, "the dawning of a brighter day majestic [would rise] on the world."[8]

I bear solemn witness to these supernal truths.

NOTES

1. *The Oxford Illustrated History of Christianity*, 6.
2. See *Teachings of Presidents of the Church: Brigham Young*, 139.
3. Quoted by Tyler in *Incidents of Experience*, in *Scraps of Biography*, 33.
4. *History of the Church*, 2:487–88.
5. *Deseret News*, 2 April 1856, 26; see also *History of the Church*, 3:385.
6. *History of the Church*, 4:165–66.
7. *History of the Church*, 3:385; emphasis in original.
8. "The Morning Breaks," *Hymns*, no. 1.

FACTORS LEADING PERSONS TO REJECT GOD

Problem	Some Scriptural References
The "Natural Man," Characteristics of	Mosiah 3:19
Unrepented Sexual Sin	Genesis 35:22; Deuteronomy 22:25; Proverbs 7:10; Matthew 5:19, 28; 3 Nephi 12:28; Colossians 3:5; Alma 39:5
Divisions, Lack of Unity, Contention	Acts 15:2, 37–39; 1 Corinthians 1:12–13; 2 Corinthians 13:11; Ephesians 4:3; 1 Peter 3:8; 2 Nephi 28:4
Love of Power	D&C 121
Fault Finding, Lack of Forgiveness	D&C 64:8, 10; James 3:14
Idolatry, Worshiping False Gods	Exodus 20:3; Leviticus 26:1; Daniel 5:23; Acts 17:29; Matthew 6:24; Romans 1:25; 1 Corinthians 8:4; Revelation 13:4; 2 Nephi 9:37; Alma 1:32; Helaman 6:31; Moses 1:15, 6:49; D&C 1:16

BIBLIOGRAPHY

Anderson, Richard Lloyd. *Understanding Paul.* Salt Lake City: Deseret Book Co., 1983.

Aurelius, Marcus. *Meditations.* Translated by Maxwell Staniforth. London: The Folio Society, 2002.

Barker, Margaret. *The Great High Priest: The Temple Roots of Christian Liturgy.* New York: T. & T. Clark, 2003.

Barnes, Timothy D. *Constantine and Eusebius.* Cambridge, Mass.: Harvard University Press, 1981.

Brown, Raymond E., and John P. Meier, *Antioch and Rome: New Testament Cradles of Catholic Christianity.* New York: Paulist Press, 1983.

Cannon, George Q. *Gospel Truth.* Edited by Jerreld L. Newquist. Salt Lake City: Deseret Book Co., 1974.

Cantor, Norman F. *The Civilization of the Middle Ages: A Completely Revised and Expanded Edition of Medieval History.* New York: HarperCollins Publishers, 1993.

Chadwick, Henry. *The Early Church.* Rev. ed. London: Penguin Books, 1993.

Cullmann, Oscar. *Peter: Disciple, Apostle, Martyr: A Historical and Theological Study.* Translated by Floyd V. Filson. 2d ed. Philadelphia: Westminster Press, 1962.

Deseret News, 2 April 1856, 26.

Documents of the Christian Church. Edited by Henry Bettenson. 2d ed. New York: Oxford University Press, 1963.

Durant, Will. *Caesar and Christ: A History of Roman Civilization and of Christianity from Their Beginnings to A.D. 325.* New York: MJF Books, 1944.

The Early Christian Fathers. Edited and translated by Henry Bettenson. London: Oxford University Press, 1969.

The Eerdmans Bible Dictionary. Grand Rapids, Mich.: William B. Eerdmans Publishing Co., 1987.

Ehrman, Bart D. *The Orthodox Corruption of Scripture: The Effect of Early Christological Controversies on the Text of the New Testament.* New York: Oxford University Press, 1993.

Encyclopedia of Early Christianity. Edited by Everett Ferguson. New York: Garland Pub. Inc., 1990.

"Epistle of Clement of Rome." In *The Apostolic Fathers.* Vol. 1. London: Griffith, Farran, Browne, & Co. Ltd., 1890.

Eusebius, *The History of the Church from Christ to Constantine.* Translated by G. A. Williamson. Rev. ed. New York: Penguin Books, 1989.

Faulconer, James E. "The Concept of Apostasy in the New Testament." Unpublished manuscript, Brigham Young University, 2002.

Faust, James E. "Keeping Covenants and Honoring the Priesthood." *Ensign,* November 1993, 36–39.

Fox, Robin Lane. *Pagans and Christians.* New York: Alfred A. Knopf, Inc., 1989.

Frend, W. H. C. *The Rise of Christianity.* Philadelphia: Fortress Press, 1984.

Gee, John. "The Corruption of Scripture in the Second Century." Unpublished manuscript, 2003.

Gibbon, Edward. *The History of the Decline and Fall of the Roman Empire.* Edited by Betty Radice, 4 vols. London: The Folio Society, 1983–86.

Green, Peter. *Alexander of Macedon, 356–323 B.C.: A Historical Biography.* Berkeley, Calif.: University of California Press, 1991.

Griffin, Carl W., and David L. Paulsen. "Augustine and the Corporeality of God." *Harvard Theological Review* 95, no. 1 (1990): 97–118.

Hatch, Edwin. *The Influence of Greek Ideas and Usage upon the Christian Church.* Edited by A. M. Fairbairn. London: Williams and Norgate, 1907.

Hinckley, Gordon B. "Priesthood Restoration." *Ensign,* October 1988, 69–72.

———. "What Are People Asking about Us?" *Ensign,* November 1998, 70–72.

Hollister, C. Warren. *Medieval Europe: A Short History.* 3rd ed. New York: John Wiley and Sons, 1974.

Irenaeus, *Contra Haereses.* In *The Ante-Nicean Fathers.* Edited by

Alexander Roberts and James Donaldson. Vol. 1. Grand Rapids, Mich.: Wm. B. Eerdmans Publishing, 1950–63.

Johnson, Paul. *A History of Christianity.* New York: Simon & Schuster, 1976.

Josephus, *The Wars of the Jews.* In *The Works of Josephus.* Translated by William Whiston. Peabody, Mass.: Hendrickson Pub., 1987.

Journal of Discourses. 26 vols. Liverpool: Latter-day Saints' Book Depot, 1854–86.

Le Goff, Jacques. *Medieval Civilization 400–1500.* Translated by Julia Barrow. New York: Barnes and Noble, 2000.

Lee, Harold B. In Conference Report, April 1953.

Lyon, T. Edgar. *Apostasy to Restoration.* Salt Lake City: Deseret Book Co., 1960.

Manchester, William. *A World Lit Only by Fire: The Medieval Mind and the Renaissance.* Boston: Little, Brown and Co., 1992.

Massie, Robert K. *Peter the Great: His Life and World.* New York: Ballantine Books, 1980.

McKay, John P., Bennett D. Hill, John Buckler, and Patricia B. Ebrey. *A History of World Societies, Vol. 1 to 1715.* Boston: Houghton Mifflin Co., 2000.

McNeill, William H. *Plagues and Peoples.* Garden City, N.Y.: Anchor Press/Doubleday, 1976.

Meeks, Wayne A. *The First Urban Christians: The Social World of the Apostle Paul.* New Haven, Conn.: Yale University Press, 1983.

———. *The Moral World of the First Christians.* Philadelphia: The Westminster Press, 1986.

"The Morning Breaks." In *Hymns.* Salt Lake City: The Church of Jesus Christ of Latter-day Saints, 1985.

Mosheim, John Laurence. *An Ecclesiastical History, Ancient and Modern.* 2 vols. Baltimore, Md.: John J. Harrod, 1832.

Norwich, John Julius. *A Short History of Byzantium.* New York: Vintage Books, 1997.

O'Shea, Stephen. *The Perfect Heresy: The Revolutionary Life and Death of the Medieval Cathars.* New York: Walker and Co., 2000.

Oaks, Dallin H. "Apostasy and Restoration." *Ensign,* May 1995, 84–87.

Olson, Roger E. *The Story of Christian Theology: Twenty Centuries of Tradition and Reform.* Downers Grove, Ill.: InterVarsity Press, 1999.

The Oxford Dictionary of Quotations. 3rd ed. New York: Oxford University Press, 1987.

The Oxford Dictionary of the Christian Church. Edited by F. L. Cross. London: Oxford University Press, 1958.

The Oxford Illustrated History of Christianity. Edited by John McManners. London: Oxford University Press, 1992.

Pagels, Elaine. *Beyond Belief: The Secret Gospel of Thomas.* New York: Random House, 2003.

Paulsen, David L. "Early Christian Belief in a Corporeal Deity: Origen and Augustine as Reluctant Witnessess." *Harvard Theological Review* 83, no. 2 (1990): 105–16.

———. "The God of Primitive Christianity: Apostasy and Restoration." Unpublished manuscript, 9 September 2002.

———. "Must God Be Incorporeal?" *Faith and Philosophy* 6, no. 1. (1989): 76–87.

Phillips, J. B. *The Young Church in Action.* London: Collins, 1955.

Reynolds, Noel B., ed. *LDS Perspectives on the Apostasy.* Provo, UT: FARMS, forthcoming, 2005.

Roberts, B. H. *Outlines of Ecclesiastical History.* Salt Lake City: George Q. Cannon and Sons Co., 1893.

Robinson, Stephen E. "Warring Against the Saints of God." *Ensign,* January 1988, 34–39.

Romer, John. *Testament: The Bible and History.* New York: Henry Holt and Co., 1988.

Rubenstein, Richard E. *When Jesus Became God: The Struggle to Define Christianity during the Last Days of Rome.* New York: Harcourt, Inc., 1999.

"St. Ignatius's Epistle to the Trallians." In *The Apostolic Fathers.* Vol. 2. London: Griffith, Farran, & Co. Ltd., 1890.

Smith, Joseph. *History of The Church of Jesus Christ of Latter-day Saints.* Edited by B. H. Roberts. 2d ed. rev. 7 vols. Salt Lake City: The Church of Jesus Christ of Latter-day Saints, 1932–51.

Sordi, Marta. *The Christians and the Roman Empire.* Translated by Annabel Bedini. London: Routledge, 1994.

Sperry, Sidney B. *Paul's Life and Letters.* Salt Lake City: Bookcraft, 1955.

Stark, Rodney. *The Rise of Christianity: A Sociologist Reconsiders History.* Princeton, N.J.: Princeton University Press, 1996.

Talmage, James E. *The Great Apostasy.* Salt Lake City: Deseret Book Co., 1968.

———. *A Study of the Articles of Faith.* Salt Lake City: Deseret Book Co., 1988.

Teachings of Presidents of the Church: Brigham Young. Salt Lake City: The Church of Jesus Christ of Latter-day Saints, 1997.

Teachings of Presidents of the Church: John Taylor. Salt Lake City: The Church of Jesus Christ of Latter-day Saints, 2001.

Tertullian. In *The Ante-Nicean Fathers*. Edited by Alexander Roberts and James Donaldson. Vol. 3. Grand Rapids, Mich.: Wm. B. Eerdmans Publishing, 1950–63.

———. *On Prescription Against Heretics*. In *The Ante-Nicean Fathers*. Edited by Alexander Roberts and James Donaldson. Vol. 3. Grand Rapids, Mich.: Wm. B. Eerdmans Publishing, 1950–63.

Times and Seasons (15 October 1841): 578.

Tuchman, Barbara W. *The March of Folly: From Troy to Vietnam*. New York: Ballantine Books, 1984.

Tyler, Daniel. In *Incidents of Experience*. In *Scraps of Biography*. Salt Lake City: Juvenile Instructor Office, 1883.

Wiles, Maurice. *The Making of Christian Doctrine: A Study in the Principles of Early Doctrinal Development*. London: Cambridge University Press, 1967.

Wills, Garry. *Papal Sin: Structures of Deceit*. New York: Doubleday, 2000.

INDEX

Abraham, 9, 25
Acton, Lord, 144
Acts, book of, 21
Adam, 8, 9
Adultery. *See* Sexual immorality
Albigensians, 158–59
Alexander, bishop of Alexandria, 116, 118
Alexander the Great, 20, 26
Alexandria, 20, 22, 25
Allegory, 73–74, 124
Alma, 73
Amaury, Arnold, 159
Ammianus, 131
Andrew, 55
Antioch, 20–21
Apocryphal writings, 6, 77, 81, 171
Apollo, 30
Apollos, 17
Apostasy: as turning against God, 6–7; cycle of, 7; will not destroy this dispensation, 11; individual, 11–13, 54, 168, 170; institutional, 13, 163–64, 168; as breaking of everlasting covenant, 36; beginnings of, 37, 45; hallmarks of, 43–44; Joseph Smith on, 45–47; and loss of priesthood authority, 50

Apostasy, Great: scriptural predictions of, 1–2, 43–44; and judging, 4; meaning of, 6; reality of, 6, 163–64, 168; Paul prophesies of, 37–38, 41–42; Judaizers and, 39; as result of internal rebellion, 42, 44–45, 165, 171; occurred quickly, 71, 125, 165

Apostles: necessary in kingdom of God, 54; hold keys of priesthood, 55; succession of, 56; Ignatius on, 56–57; in latter-day church, 166–67

Apostles, early: take sacrament, 10; preach in urban areas, 22; death of, 51; chosen by Christ, 54–55; names of, 55; filling vacancy in quorum of, 55–56; vague records about, 56, 58, 66; bishops and, 57; Gnostic beliefs about, 148; warn saints about dissension, 165. *See also* Paul; Peter

181